Promptings OR ME?

Recognizing THE SPIRIT'S VOICE

Promptings OR ME?

Recognizing THE SPIRIT'S VOICE

KEVIN HINCKLEY

M.ED LPC

CFI
SPRINGVILLE, UTAH

ISBN 13: 978-1-59955-490-7

Published by CFI, an imprint of Cedar Fort, Inc., 2373 W. 700 S., Springville, UT 84663
Distributed by Cedar Fort, Inc., www.cedarfort.com

LIBRARY OF CONGRESS CATALOGING-IN-PUBLICATION DATA

Hinckley, Kevin.
  Promptings or me? / Kevin Hinckley.
    p. cm.
  Includes bibliographical references.
  ISBN 978-1-59955-490-7
  1. Prayer--Church of Jesus Christ of Latter-day Saints. 2.
Inspiration--Religious aspects--Church of Jesus Christ of Latter day Saints.
  3. Church of Jesus Christ of Latter-day Saints--Doctrines. I. Title.
  BV210.3.H56 2010
  248.3'2--dc22

                        2010039188

Cover design by Megan Whittier
Cover design © 2011 by Lyle Mortimer
Edited and typeset by Kelley Konzak

Printed in the United States of America

10 9 8 7 6 5 4 3 2 1

Printed on acid-free paper

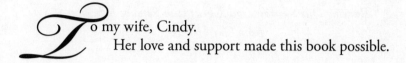To my wife, Cindy.
Her love and support made this book possible.

OTHER BOOKS BY KEVIN HINCKLEY

*Parenting the Strong-Willed Child: Fortifying Our Youth
and Healing Our Prodigals*

*Burying Our Swords: How Christ Can Remove Rebellion
from Our Hearts*

table of contents

preface

As a boy, the Prophet Joseph Smith watched his parents deal with the constant life and death struggles of a family in rural New England. In particular, he watched his mother retire to the woods to pray for answers and comfort during difficult times. He heard his father pray intently over the family and teach from the Bible at night. Years later, he followed their example when he sought his own answers from the Lord. As we read of his experience in the Sacred Grove, we are reminded that everything good begins by seeking answers from our Heavenly Father.

The history of Adam's seed, righteous and wicked, is filled with a constant search for answers. We all want to know how to solve the difficult problems. The closer we draw to the Lord, the more we recognize our need for divine help. We pray for Church and government leaders. We approach the Lord, looking for comfort during tragedy. We kneel in gratitude to give thanks for blessings received.

Then there are those puzzling times when there appear to be no answers to our heavenly petitions, as though the leaden heavens have become "as brass," and we are left to wonder what happened. In response, we may question ourselves, our approach, or even our own worthiness. "Did I pray the 'right' way?" We wonder. "Did I pray long enough?" "Did I ask for the wrong things?" "Am I being punished for past sins?" "Is the Lord just letting me struggle so that I can learn an important lesson?" "Perhaps he simply doesn't care about this decision and so I'm supposed to figure it out."

A few years ago I spoke at a singles' conference on this topic. A man came up afterward and said earnestly, "Brother Hinckley, I have been married and divorced four times. Each time I prayed to know if it was the right decision to get married. Each time I felt I received a positive answer. And each marriage was a disaster! Why can't I get it right? What is wrong with me?"

As with this good brother, we can easily become discouraged when we follow what we believe to be the promptings of the Spirit, only to have the results turn out much more negative than we planned. "Did I really feel the Spirit?" we ask. "Did I understand it correctly?" "If I had used a different set of words, would it have changed the results?" "Was I supposed to fast and didn't?" "I wonder if I simply heard what I wanted to hear." "Is there a lesson in this I'm supposed to learn and I'm just missing it?"

As a result, most of us, at one time or another, find ourselves standing at a decision crossroads. "Two paths diverged in a wood . . ."[1] We look carefully at potential paths. Unfortunately, we can see only the first portion of each path before it disappears into the woods. We have little or no idea where each path will lead. We are aware, however, that each path will probably result in drastically different results and could change our lives completely. The longer we stand at this crossroads, the longer we fear making the wrong decision.

So, given the long-term impact of difficult decisions, we crave divine confirmation from One much smarter than we are. But when that confirmation is delayed or doesn't come, we sit at that crossroads, staring out at the two paths.

To be fair, however, our presence at the crossroads says a lot about our faith in God. It is faith that leads us to trust that He has the answers we need. We've successfully gotten answers before and probably know family and friends who have as well. So, in faith and by experience, we turn to the Lord to know which path to take.

Thus it is that all of us, at different points in our lives, end up pleading and listening, searching for words, whisperings, feelings, or anything that will move us off the crossroads and down the right road.

At those moments, it is critical that we remember that our Heavenly Father loves us. As our young women repeat, "we are [children] of our Heavenly Father, who loves us, and we love Him."[2] We also know that it is the Lord's intent that we seek Him out for answers to life's decisions. "I am the living water," the Savior explains to the Samaritan woman. He told her that those who drink that water—His water—would never thirst again (see John 4:1–14). He didn't intend for us to walk these paths alone, and He has promised not to abandon us. It isn't in His nature.

It is also true that honing and developing spiritual sensitivities takes effort and experience. King Benjamin warned that the natural, or fallen, man is "an enemy to God . . . and will be, forever and ever" (Mosiah 3:19). As we'll discuss in chapter one, the superficial prayers of the natural man and woman are always ineffective because they seek for things to "consume it upon [their] lust." Also, true to form, the natural man will turn to God only in his hour of need, primarily seeking for things to be "fixed" and then returning to his old ways as soon as possible.

President Howard W. Hunter once observed:

"If prayer is only a spasmodic cry at the time of crisis, then it is utterly selfish and we come to think of God as a repairman or a service agency to help us only in our emergencies. We should remember the Most High day and night—always—not only at times when all other assistance has failed and we desperately need help."[3]

This vital process, then, of growing and developing our tender spiritual sensitivities is the same process needed to "cast off" the natural man and become "as a child." Young children are teachable and obedient. They generally obey the counsel of their parents. Adults who come to Christ are likewise taught to develop a "broken heart and contrite spirit." The meek desire (crave!) divine guidance, seeking and searching, listening and pondering. They also experience great joy when sacred counsel finally arrives.

Finally, I believe that most active Latter-day Saints strive each day to walk the "peaceable walk with the children of men" (Moroni 7:4). We accept callings in the Church and strive to raise our children in the gospel. We sin and we repent. We try our best to stay true to the covenants we've made with the Lord.

However, regardless of all our obedience, we're still not quite sure how to access heaven in a way that removes all doubt as to the source of our answers and the direction we're to go. We are, as one leader confided, "spiritually illiterate."[4] It could be that we don't know exactly what to look for. Or that we tend to shrink from counsel we didn't expect. And some of us, unfortunately, pray diligently for guidance, receive wonderful answers, and then let other people talk us out of following the answer we've received.

In short, spiritual direction from a loving Father flows to well-meaning people every day. Our responsibility is to prepare our hearts to hear it. Will we have the courage to follow the answers we get? Will we be able to distinguish those answers from our own thoughts and Satan's deceitfulness? Or will we remain frozen at the crossroads?

To which the Savior beckons: "Come, and see!"

Notes

1. Robert Frost, "The Road Not Taken."
2. "Young Women Theme," *Young Women Personal Progress: Standing As a Witness of God* (booklet, 2001), 5.
3. Clyde J. Williams, ed., *The Teachings of Howard W. Hunter, Fourteenth President of the Church of Jesus Christ of Latter-day Saints* (Salt Lake City: Bookcraft, 1997), 38–39.
4. F. Enzio Busche, "Unleashing the Dormant Spirit," BYU Devotional, May 14, 1996, 2.

chapter one

WHAT I PRAY FOR

I PRAY BECAUSE I CAN'T HELP MYSELF. I PRAY BECAUSE I'M HELP-
LESS. I PRAY BECAUSE THE NEED FLOWS OUT OF ME ALL THE TIME,
WAKING AND SLEEPING. IT DOESN'T CHANGE GOD; IT CHANGES ME.
C. S. LEWIS

O kay now, honey, push!" Mike pleaded gently. Wearily, Judy
nodded and drew in her breath for one last try.

"That's great," said the doctor, glancing over at her, "just
one last push. I can see the head. You can do it!"

With one last effort, Judy pushed with all her might. Mike watched
excitedly as their new baby emerged and then slid easily into the doctor's waiting arms.

"It's a boy!" The nurse beamed. "A beautiful little boy."

Judy quickly glanced over at Mike, who stared with disbelief at
his new son. *A-another boy?* he thought. *It can't be!* He looked back at
Judy, who managed a weak smile and a quick shrug before she lay back,
exhausted.

Later that night, Mike drove home, deep in thought and filled
with confusion. Another boy! He pictured their five other boys. He
and Judy loved every one of them. But year after year Judy had longed
for a little girl. Financially, things had been difficult for his growing
family. Mike had been worried about affording another child but also
believed that the Lord would take care of them if they felt inspired to
have another one.

He remembered that morning, a year ago, when Judy had awakened with a big smile.

"Mike," she'd said as she shook him awake, "let me tell you about my dream!"

He'd sat up groggily, trying to clear his head and listen to her excitement.

"I saw her!" Judy had breathed. "I dreamt about her. Mike, I saw our little girl. She's beautiful, and she wants to be here!"

Seeing the look of confusion on Mike's face, Judy had leaned over and gently taken his hand. "I had a dream or a vision or something. I was out walking in a field, and all of a sudden I saw her. She was about five years old, and she just stood there, smiling and waving at me. It was the most peaceful feeling I've ever had. I know—I *know*—we are supposed to have one more. She's up there waiting to come down."

As Mike drove through the quiet city, he shook his head again. After her dream, they had prayed about it. And, despite all the bills and demands of five active boys, they agreed they were being prompted to invite their little girl to join them.

Mike's confusion kept building. Judy had described feeling so peaceful following her dream. And he had to admit he felt good also. They'd believed they were being prompted to finally have the little girl Judy wanted so much. In fact, they were so certain, they hadn't even wanted to know the results of the sonogram, which would have told them for sure.

Why would the Lord do this to her? Mike questioned. *To us? Why?*

As Latter-day Saints, we desire to have close, ongoing relationships with our Creator. Instinctively, we know He is the source of guidance, of answers. Beyond that, the more we understand the true nature of the Father/child relationship, the more we look to our Heavenly Parent to give us comfort and counsel in a place far removed from our original home. Reaching upward is a natural act, a desire to find the safety and reassurance we knew in another time and place.

Partly because of those expectations, however, we become concerned when needed answers are slow in coming or when we feel we've gotten an answer and have followed it, only to run into disaster.

Recently, a client came into my office in tears. The mother of a young family, she is married to a man who is depressed and unwilling to receive any treatment. As a result, he loses one job after another and has now been unemployed for several years. Most of his days consist of sitting on the living room couch and staring gloomily at the TV. A couple of years ago, my client, fearing that her husband's condition would not get any better, went out and got additional certifications that resulted in her finding a very good job. Several months ago, she was laid off, but because of her skills and experience, she knows she will have no problem finding another job.

"Then why the tears?" I asked. "You are good at what you do, and finding another place to work doesn't seem to be the problem."

She slowly shook her head. "I know I'm good at what I do. I already have a couple of job offers. But for years, I've hated it. My stomach churns every morning before work. And I really dread going back. I kept hoping my husband would go back to work so I wouldn't have to, but he won't. If I don't go back, we're going to be in financial trouble."

She then admitted to praying for long hours, desperately trying to get confirmation between two job offers. Her tears flowed more freely as she described being unable to feel good about either option, both of which would have her returning to an industry she dreads.

"But," she sighed, "what else can I do? No one else is going to give us the benefits or the income we need. I don't want to go back and can't get an answer either. What am I supposed to do?"

In response, I requested permission to ask a series of questions. She agreed.

"First of all, is God our Heavenly Father?" I asked.

She smiled for the first time and quickly nodded. "Of course," she responded.

"Does He love us?

"Yes."

"Does He want us to be happy?"

Again she nodded her head yes.

"Does He know us and know our needs?"

Again she smiled. "I know He does," she returned firmly.

"Does He know what will happen to us in the future?" I then asked.

"Sure, he's God!"

"Okay," I then asked, "if Heavenly Father knows us and loves us and wants us to be happy, if he knows our needs and what will happen to us in the future, then what, exactly, are you praying about?"

3

She was quiet as she thought about my question.

"As I understand it," I continued, "you are in a position, like it or not, where you have to work. You've narrowed down your choices to two companies, neither of which you like. Yet you've been trying to convince the Lord to tell you which of those companies you should work for, given that they have the best benefits and highest wages. They are *your* best options. Are they the Lord's?"

After a moment, she asked softly, "Okay, then what *am* I supposed to be asking for?"

For each of us, that is the critical question. Imagine, if you will, standing before a great chef at a world famous restaurant. Seeking his advice, you explain, "I'm trying to cook a gourmet meal for some very special guests. Should I cook up the beanie weenie or the spam surprise? Which would be the best choice?" If we did have the chance to get a recommendation from a famous chef, would we seek to limit him or her to the two choices *we* could think up, based on our limited experience, or would we instead want him or her to give us the benefit of his or her experience and knowledge, perhaps suggesting things we've never thought of. In other words, would we want to choose from our limited set of possibilities or from the vast array of options based on the chef's experience?

As a child of God, I'm given the blessing of kneeling each night—and any other time I choose—before the Creator of the universe. He holds all things in His hands. He also knows, intimately, my wants, my needs, and my future. In addition, I've felt His love on too many occasions to doubt how He feels about me. It is for this reason that when I have a problem, I'm much more interested in His solutions than mine!

Part of the difficulty with presenting my own solutions to God is my natural-man shortsightedness. I suffer from the same myopic problem most of us struggle with; that is, we think we know what we want and need, but we may be completely wrong. This is why President Joseph F. Smith warned us that "the education of our desires is one of far-reaching importance to our happiness in life."[1]

To put it differently, I only *think* I know what I want and need. What I think I want is bound up in short-term desires and limited by the blinders of my personal experiences. Like a child, I can see only so far into my future, and I plan accordingly. What the Lord sees for me stretches into the eternities. Therefore, His guidance and direction take into consideration all that I can be, not just what I want at the moment, given my restricted view of myself.

Elder Neal A. Maxwell wisely pointed out:

> Even though we may ask in faith for something, unless it is right for us, God reserves the decision-making power to himself. A perfect, loving, and omniscient Father would do just that. Thus, in addition to having faith, *we need to ask for that which is right.*
>
> Clearly, the Lord reserves the right to determine that which is best for us, lest we ask for something in our spiritual naïveté that would not conform to the will of God.
>
> Nephi, the prophet, understood the importance of precision and propriety in prayer. He knew from happy experience that God would give liberally to him if he, Nephi, *prayed in such a way that he "ask not amiss."*[2]

When I rely on my own wisdom in the things I ask for, I am very likely to ask "amiss." I don't yet know exactly what I *really* need, only what I think I need or want.

As a teenager, one of our sons wanted a certain wristwatch for Christmas. It was all he could think about. He had gone down to the watch store, tried one on, and imagined just how much fun it would be to own one. In the weeks leading up to the holidays, any discussion about what he wanted started with that watch.

That year, as a gift to our children, we decided to pin a certain amount of money to the Christmas tree for each child and then go down to the mall the day after Christmas and let everyone pick out whatever they wanted with their own money. On Christmas morning, my son gleefully pulled his money off the tree, realizing that the watch he wanted would take most of the money he'd received but that he'd finally be able to get it.

The next day, when we arrived at the mall, he went straight to the store and eagerly bought his new watch. For days afterward, he showed it to family and friends. He wore it proudly to church. However, before a week had passed, he had taken it back to the store for a refund, bought a few other things he also wanted, and saved the rest of his gift money. Only after getting his dream watch did he realize there were other things he wanted more.

Again, we can be lulled into thinking we know what we want and need and then try to convince the Lord to assist us with our limited view of ourselves. However, don't we really want to know what He wants for us? If so, pure and meaningful dialogue with heaven should be focused on learning His mind and will while surrendering our own myopic agenda.

The Bible Dictionary explains it this way:

> Prayer is the act by which the will of the Father and the will of the child are brought into correspondence with each other. *The object of prayer is not to change the will of God,* but to secure for ourselves and for others blessings that God is already willing to grant, but that are made conditional on our asking for them. . . .
>
> We pray in Christ's name when our mind is the mind of Christ, and our wishes the wishes of Christ. . . . *We then ask for things it is possible for God to grant.* (Bible Dictionary, p. 752–53, emphasis added)

If I ask for things only according to my "natural-man agenda," it appears as though I place Heavenly Father in a bind. By asking for things I want but clearly aren't right for me, I place the God of heaven, who knows my needs much more clearly, in the position of having to refuse my request, for I'm asking that in granting my feeble desire, he grant things I don't need or that might really hurt me.

It is for these reasons, then, that our purpose in prayer must not be to change the will of God or to try to convince Him with what we consider well-constructed logic or with endless emotional pleadings. Our desire must be to learn His mind and will and seek for the faith to carry it out. It really is that simple.

As I explained all this to my young friend, she agreed to everything we'd talked about. "But," she said after a minute, "what *am* I supposed to be praying about then? Am I not supposed to ask for anything?"

And with that, she reached the crucial crossroads in gaining answers to prayers. If I conclude that I would rather rely on the Lord's wisdom as opposed to mine, then I have to conclude that much of what I often say in my prayers still focuses most on what I think I need.

My natural man has a long list of things he wants. When he prays, he wants it done *his* way and on *his* timetable. Those prayers can ring pretty hollow. However, when I'm able to temper his demands, my prayers sound—and feel—completely different.

During those times when I am meek and submissive, I am more focused on the things He wants for me. It is during those times that I acknowledge that I need help and guidance, that I desire to learn what the Lord would have me do, and that I would be willing to follow whatever course he might dictate.

It is also during those times I let the Holy Ghost "teach [me] all things" I should say. When I asked my young client if she'd ever had an experience where the Spirit had inspired her while giving a talk or bearing her testimony, she readily acknowledged that she had. Most of us, in fact, have had moments during a class or talk when we hear ourselves speak with an eloquence we do not have otherwise. In those moments we learn doctrine as we are speaking it and we are taught along with the congregation.

Effective prayers work in a similar way. When I am submissive and willing to follow any divine guidance I might receive, I place myself in a position to be guided and prompted, not just in what I should do but also in what I am to pray for. At those moments it is not unusual to hear myself asking the Lord for things I didn't even know I needed.

Natural Man Prayers	Meekness Prayers
What I want is . . .	Thank you
What I need is . . .	Give me ears to hear
I've got to have . . .	As I submit, please remove my weaknesses
Please change this . . .	What is it I'm to do?
	Help Thou my unbelief

Certainly, there is nothing wrong with asking the Lord for something we or a loved one needs. That is part of why we pray. However, we need to be careful to let the Spirit help *dictate* those pleadings. When we do that, we bring inspired options to the Lord to be confirmed. He will teach us what to pray for and then confirm those choices.

My client realized she didn't have the ability to cause an immediate change on her husband. Certainly, the financial responsibility for the family would continue to rest on her. She also knew that despite her experience and formal training, she could not feel good about going back to the industry that made the most logical sense. She *knew* that. She also realized that pleading with the Lord that He would sanction one of her dreaded decisions had not worked.

Prayer Experiment

What I suggested to my client was a prayer experiment.

"I'm sure that in a Church talk or class you've heard someone suggest that you can have a great prayer experience if, even just once, while praying, you don't ask for anything. Instead, you state all the things you are grateful for and then finish."

She nodded her head yes. Most of us have heard or tried something similar.

"Here's my challenge," I went on. "Do that all the time. Simply tell Heavenly Father how grateful you are for everything you do have, everything you've been given, and for all the little 'tender mercies' he's given you over time. Ask His forgiveness for things you've done wrong. Then explain to Him your concerns and worries and desires. When you've done that, simply listen and pay attention to any direction you feel flowing into your heart and mind. Continue to listen during the day—when you are driving, when you're at the store, and when you take a walk. Stay in tune and leave your heart open to His guidance."

"I can do that," she returned with a smile. "But it will be strange trying to pray without asking for anything."

I quickly agreed that it can be a little strange at first. I admitted that my natural man is fearful that if I don't tell him everything—if I leave something off the list—then somehow He won't know, as though the God of heaven is ignorant of or unwilling to grant me my needs until I tell them to Him. But I need to be constantly reminded that He does know my needs—better than I do. That's the point. *He is trying to educate me, not the other way around.* The sooner I surrender my need to do things *my way*, the sooner I put myself in a place to be guided *his way.* Certainly there are some blessings that are contingent upon our asking. However, as we listen closely to the Spirit, we will be taught which ones we should be asking for.

The prayer challenge can be a little awkward at first. We are trained—conditioned—to lay out a long list of things we feel we need. I once had a Church leader who typed out a long agenda of things to talk to God about. He feared leaving things out, worrying that inspiration would not come if he forgot something. Again, we are to take to the Lord those things we're concerned about. We are to lay those things at His feet.

We all struggle with this, often laying out our worries and then telling Heavenly Father how and when and where to "fix" them. When we do so, we tend to believe our prayers have been "answered" because the results match exactly what we asked for. "I asked; I got it; it's true!" Any different result or a lack of immediate, resounding heavenly response, and we assume there was no answer or that we do not deserve to be answered.

Desires Versus Agendas

In reality, approaching the Lord in prayer is much like any search for truth: We need to be honest with ourselves as to why we want the answers we do. A professional scientist, for instance, must honestly approach his or her research with a desire to discover truth, regardless of what truth the outcome might reveal. Less-than-ethical scientists, on the other hand, begin their search with an agenda or outcome already in mind. They might hope to uncover facts that appear to confirm a theory or support the person or company funding their research. In other words, they don't really want the truth, they only want facts that support their theories.

In the very same way, we must be honest about what it is we really desire. Knowledge from God—guidance, direction, answers—almost always requires action on our part. We are responsible for the knowledge we receive, and He expects us to act on that information. If we do not, we are not only guilty of disobedience, but we also place future revelations in jeopardy as well.

During moments of the deepest honesty, we might also be forced to admit we have developed some fervently held agendas we may or may not be aware of. For instance, we might be very comfortable living the life we are living and—in our heart of hearts—not want heavenly inspiration telling us we'll have to do something different. We might have already decided the things we want to do and are fearful the Lord will have us do something else.

A young mother I know began her marriage planning on having a set amount of children. I do not know how she decided on the large number she did, but she and her husband began to faithfully have a baby each year in order to reach the ultimate goal. With each passing year, their meager finances became less and less adequate to meet their growing needs. Any attempts by wise Church leaders to suggest curtailing or slowing the growth of their family was met with a firm, "I prayed about it, and this is what the Lord wants us to do."

Ultimately, these young parents are the only ones who know if the "inspiration" they believe they've had is of the Lord. They should be concerned, though, when caring Church leaders, who've also had keys of stewardship given them, are feeling otherwise. They would do well to make sure that their personal agendas aren't influencing the internal voices they're listening to.

At such moments, we do not really want answers (though we might think we do); we only want confirmations of our preset, predetermined agendas. When we limit ourselves in this way, we take the slightest spiritual inkling or stirring of emotion as divine confirmation. We then move forward, boldly declaring our actions as God's will.

It is for these reasons that we should begin our search for guidance with a simple question: What are my agendas? If we can respond that all we want is whatever God wants, we are then open to any and all options He has for us.

Notes

1. Joseph F. Smith, *Gospel Doctrine*, 5th ed. (Salt Lake City: Deseret Book, 1939), 297.
2. Neal A. Maxwell, "What Should We Pray For?" in Spencer W. Kimball et al., *Prayer* (Salt Lake City: Deseret Book, 1979), 44.

chapter two

WHAT WE KNOW FOR SURE

THE WORD OF GOD HIDDEN IN THE HEART IS A STUBBORN
VOICE TO SUPPRESS.

BILLY GRAHAM

*I*n 1938 J. Reuben Clark was called to be a member of the first Presidency. One of his first assignments was to speak to the Church Education teachers gathered at Aspen Grove above Provo for their annual retreat. His landmark address to that group, called "The Charted Course of the Church in Education," was a clarion call to Church educators to build testimonies among their students and to avoid mixing in the philosophies of the world. President Clark began with a quote from Daniel Webster, given during a debate in the US Senate. Mr. Webster stated:

> When the mariner has been tossed for many days in thick weather, and on an unknown sea, he naturally avails himself of the first pause in the storm, the earliest glance of the sun, to take his latitude, and ascertain how far the elements have driven him from his true course. Let us imitate this prudence, and, before we float farther on the waves of this debate, refer to the point from which we departed, that we may at least be able to conjecture where we now are.[1]

In our lives we may find ourselves struggling for answers to life's questions and wondering how to proceed. Personal storms can feel unrelenting. During these periodic storms, if we are not careful, we

11

can be blown far off our intended course. When that happens, we can reclaim our proper heading by taking the time to examine our present location and then plot a better course.

When faced with stormy weather, I can begin my course correction by asking, "What do I know for sure?" Certainly, there are always unknowns and factors I cannot control. It is comforting, though, to begin with things I know I can count on. What I know for sure gives a fixed location from which to plot a new course across unknown waters.

Our search for answers should begin with prayer. Confirming divine answers hinges on our ability to understand the source as well as the direction given. Along the way, ideas or feelings may arise, providing us with indications of the road to be followed. But then doubts may arise. We often struggle to distinguish between "still, small voices" and our own, natural-man desires. We fear we might have heard only what we wanted to hear and not necessarily what the Lord intended. This is especially true when we are faced with a crisis or pending deadline.

Sometimes, though, there appears to be no answer at all. True, we understand that the lack of response might be a simple "no." Or worse, it could be the infamous stupid (stupor) of thought! Are we just so impatient or distracted that the Holy Ghost cannot be heard? For whatever reason, nights fly by, answers do not come, and the situation grows more critical. At those moments, we understand well the Lord's disciples who cried out, "Master, we perish!" (Luke 8:24).

Prayers can bring the desired answers. But again, without knowing the source of those answers, we might still be frozen in place, still not sure which course leads to a safe harbor. At these moments, we can begin by asking, "What do I know for sure?" In other words, which truths do not change and will help provide divine bearings we can comfortably sail toward? In reviewing communication with Deity, there are at least four fundamental truths that should bring comfort and help light the way if we will let them.

1. Our Heavenly Father Loves Us

The young women of the Church are reminded of their bearings each week as they recite the Young Women Theme. It begins: "We are daughters of our Heavenly Father, who loves us, and we love him."[2]

What a beautiful statement of truth! Any discussion about prayer begins here. Heavenly Father's relationship with His children is based on His eternal love for us. "This is my work and my glory," He declares, "to bring to pass the immortality and eternal life of man" (Moses 1:39). His creations receive His complete attention because we are His entire work and glory.

The Apostle Paul knew well the persecution and trial of the early Saints. He also watched the many forces trying to destroy the Church. Many Saints, rather than give in to those forces, were losing their lives in consequence of their belief in Jesus of Nazareth. "Who shall separate us from the love of Christ?" Paul wrote to these hardy souls. "Shall tribulation, or distress, or persecution, or famine, or nakedness, or peril, or sword?" (Romans 8:35). Certainly they had experienced all those. But then he finishes with the reassurance and the reality:

> For I am persuaded, that neither death, nor life, nor angels, nor principalities, nor powers, nor things present, nor things to come,
> Nor height, nor depth, nor any other creature, shall be able to separate us from the love of God, which is in Christ Jesus our Lord. (Romans 8:38–39)

The power of Paul's declaration can give us certainty in the midst of our trials. Satan has attacked the noble and great ones from the beginning of time. Voices from Jerusalem, the Roman Colosseum, Zarahemla, and Far West can testify of his evil effectiveness. But Paul reminds us that in spite of mobs and lions, Golgotha and Carthage, Satan will eternally be unable to drive the wedge he desires between the Lord's love and His children.

As we understand the power of this divine love, our heavenly petitions burn with a brighter intensity. Certainly, the prophet Enoch was a personal witness to it. As part of his prophetic calling, he was permitted to view a sweeping panorama of the earth's history and her people. That vision, seen by all dispensational prophets, is not always pleasant. In addition to viewing the Father's creations, he also saw, in devastating detail, Noah and the widespread death caused by the Flood. He appears to be caught off guard by the depth of God's reaction to the coming cataclysm:

> And it came to pass that the God of heaven looked upon the residue [the wicked] of the people, and he wept; *and Enoch bore record of*

it, saying: How is it that the heavens weep, and shed forth their tears as the rain upon the mountains?

The Lord said unto Enoch: Behold these thy brethren; they are the workmanship of mine own hands. . . .

Wherefore, I can stretch forth mine hands and hold all the creations which I have made; *and mine eye can pierce them also*, and among all the workmanship of mine hands there has not been so great wickedness as among thy brethren. (Moses 7:28, 32, 36, emphasis added)

Eternity is filled with the Lord's creations, and the Creator knows each one individually. In a powerful way we are unable to comprehend, His eye can pierce each heart and know each desire. Enoch's grand vision showed him that the earth's immersion in water would result in the death of those most unprepared to leave mortality. In response, the heavens wept. Enoch needed to understand that with divine love often comes divine pain. Moved by the tears of God and the death of his people, he too wept and "[refused] to be comforted" (Moses 7:44).

Again, the ability of the Lord to pierce each heart and understand each trauma is impossible for mortal man or woman to comprehend. But His omniscience is as vast as is His love. Conversely, it is Satan, not God, who lies to us and tries to convince us we are forgotten and alone. Only Satan would propose that the universe is too vast and individual struggles too insignificant to catch God's eye. And only he would insist that past imperfections place us beyond the redeeming love of the Savior.

Not long ago, a depressed client sat dejectedly in my office. Bound by an obsessive need to be perfect, he struggled with the wide gap he saw between his actions and living a celestial life. All he could see was how much he had fallen short in his life and had "disappointed" God, his family, and everyone else around him. Despite his faithful obedience and constant service in his callings, he saw himself as a failure.

Finally, after listening to all his perceived shortcomings, I responded with: "And to make it worse, you don't have any faith either!"

He stared closely at me. "I don't have any faith?" he asked.

I nodded. "Given everything you do on a regular basis and how hard you strive to be the person you believe Heavenly Father expects of you, if you continue to believe God is that disappointed in you, then either you are lacking in faith or you just don't know Him very well."

He was pretty quiet when he left my office. Several weeks later he returned to say that the idea that he might lack faith had caused him to closely examine his life and how he viewed the Lord. In the process he was beginning to see how he had assumed that the Lord saw him through the same narrow lens he used to view himself.

"Okay, maybe I need to work on my faith," he concluded. And he was right. The truth was that the Lord loved him more than he could fathom. Past sins he had committed were now white as snow, and the Lord remembered them "no more." But, my friend still had some work to do in order to actually believe that.

2. He Wants Us to Pray to Him

The next unchangeable truth is that He wants his children to pray to him. "If ye would hearken unto the Spirit which teacheth a man to pray ye would know that ye must pray" (2 Nephi 32:8). This was made clear to the brother of Jared in the Book of Mormon. During the confusion of Babel, the brother of Jared approached the Lord, asking Him not to confuse the languages of his family and friends. Not only was his supplication granted, but they were also led away from the confusion of Babel and put on a path toward their promised land.

Once safe, the Jaredites were like many of us. The crisis passed, and prayers lost their urgency. What they did not yet understand was that the Lord had prepared a much grander plan for their welfare—and He was anxious for them to know about it. After four years, it was time for the brother of Jared to learn that important lesson.

"At the end of four years . . . the Lord came again unto the brother of Jared, and stood in a cloud and talked with him. And for the space of three hours did the Lord talk with the brother of Jared, *and chastened him because he remembered not to call upon the name of the Lord*" (Ether 2:14, emphasis added).

Try to imagine being chastised by the Lord for three hours. Imagine being chastised for three minutes! In this case, the reason for chastisement was very clear. "The Lord said unto him: I will forgive thee and thy brethren *of their sins*" (Ether 2:15). His sin, the cause of his chastisement, was the lack of prayer. To his eternal credit, the brother of Jared meekly learned what the Lord wanted him to know. His revelatory experience is one of the great moments in all scriptural writ. And it would not have occurred had he not prayed.

The Lord has clearly taught that prayer is a commandment and that neglecting prayers brings condemnation. We might wonder why failing to pray is a sin. As a young investigator asked, "I don't get why He needs us to praise Him in prayer. It makes it look like He has an ego problem!"

However, the Lord himself explains it through the prophet Nephi. "The Spirit of the Lord," He warns, "will not always strive with man" (2 Nephi 26:11). To neglect our prayers is to fail to call down the power of heaven in our behalf. We quit growing spiritually and are left to ourselves. Cut off from the Spirit, hearts harden and grow cold. Once in this state, covenants are forgotten and the plan of happiness becomes a distant memory. In its place, a thousand other plans compete for dominance in our hearts. As we explained to this investigator, "The Lord doesn't need it, but we do. Understanding His love is part of our being empowered by Him."

As a teen, I became determined to know the truthfulness of the Book of Mormon. Having grown up in the Church, I came to a point when I knew I couldn't continue to live on borrowed light. I wanted my own answer. An inspired seminary teacher suggested a simple approach. "Read the Book of Mormon each night for just fifteen minutes," he suggested. "But before you read, pray that its truthfulness will be manifested to you. After you read, pray again to know if what you just read was true. Pray, read, pray." He promised that if this simple plan were followed, I would get the answer I wanted. I decided to try it.

For weeks I faithfully read each night. Each night I prayed before and afterward. Each night I held myself to just fifteen minutes of reading. During those weeks, I found I was enjoying a consistent closeness to the Spirit. But still I sought a deeper confirmation. Then, one night, after I had knelt in prayer, I read from Alma: "Counsel with the Lord in all thy doings, and he will direct thee for good; yea, when thou liest down at night lie down to the Lord, that he might watch over you in your sleep; and when thou risest in the morning let thy heart be full of thanks unto God; and if ye do these things, ye shall be lifted up at the last day" (Alma 37:37).

As I read, this verse leapt off the page at me as if it were illuminated. It filled my sixteen-year-old heart to the point I could read no further. I quickly closed the book and knelt beside my bed. I asked if what I had read was true. My heart swelled within me, and I was filled with waves of joy. Those feelings lasted all that night and left me with a profound feeling of peace extending for days afterward.

Looking back, the spirit of that revelatory moment was so overwhelming that I paid very little attention to the words that prompted the outpouring. Only later did I realize the Lord's dual purpose in how He answered my prayer. I had wanted to know if the book was inspired, and that prayer was answered. But later in life, there would be other questions and other needs. And there, radiating from the page, was the loving reassurance that future prayers would also be answered. I simply needed to approach Him with the same determination as I had in gaining a testimony of the Book of Mormon.

I believe Alma deliberately chose a powerful word to describe our relationship with our Heavenly Father when we pray. "*Counsel* with the Lord . . ." he tells us, "and he will direct thee for good." We know of other scriptures that tell us "ask and you shall receive; knock and it shall be opened unto you" (D&C 4:7). To get our answers, there may be plenty of asking and knocking. But Alma explains that the Lord desires us to "counsel" with him, meaning, I take it, that we discuss, we confer, we draw guidance from He who knows what we really need.

Heavenly petitions drenched deep in counsel and discussion are far more than traditional prayer. They draw down the "powers of heaven" (3 Nephi 20:22) into our lives and shape our decisions. These communications are far more than requests to a spiritual help desk; they shape us and stretch our souls for the eternities.

3. The Divine Paradox

The next eternal truth, something we should know for sure, is the divine paradox. The divine paradox is the balancing act we maintain between our dualistic selves. On one hand, Peter describes man's divine nature and destiny by exclaiming: "ye are a chosen generation, a royal priesthood, an holy nation, a peculiar people" (1 Peter 2:9) We are aware that as children of God and part of Covenant Israel, we've been reserved for the last days and have a divine destiny. *Wow*, we think, *we are pretty special!*

On the other hand, we have King Benjamin reminding his people that they are "less than the dust of the earth" (Mosiah 4:2). Moses's Enoch-like vision left him exclaiming, "now I know that man is nothing" (Moses 1:10). Even Ammon, who watched the Lord dramatically change Lamanite hearts and behavior, was quick to remind his companions, "I do not boast in my own strength" (Alma 26:11). Or, as a client recently moaned: "I am an enemy of God!"

In other words, while we thrill at our eternal possibilities, we must also come to view ourselves as unworthy and undeserving of any blessings given to us. When being extended a difficult calling, a humble priesthood holder responded with, "But I'm not worthy!" To which his caring priesthood leader responded, "Brother, the Lord has to be merciful to allow any of us to work in His kingdom!" And so He is.

The celestial kingdom is reserved for those who are clean, but only because they have been redeemed. And that redemption does not come as anything we've earned. We've tried, fallen, repented, and fallen short again—and yet He loves us and has provided a way to return to Him.

Before we, as "noble and great ones" (Abraham 3:22), begin dancing down our divine road to exaltation, we must first recognize how dependent we are on God—for everything we are. In this sense, we are all "beggars" (see Mosiah 4:16). The Apostle Peter explains "that ye should shew forth the praises of him *who hath called you out of darkness into his marvellous light*" (1 Peter 2:9, emphasis added).

Thus, the entire plan of happiness involves understanding and marveling at the divine paradox. The many ironies include the following:

To find ourselves,

>we must first lose ourselves.

To be forgiven,

>we must first forgive.

To be filled with joy,

>we need to endure tribulation.

To be "raised up,"

>He needed first to descend below all things.

To receive an endowment of power,

>we first bind ourselves to covenants.

To achieve exaltation,

>*we must first serve.*

The greater our potential, the more intervention is needed. Godly guidance when combined with the blood of the Lamb opens the door to an endless life, or God's life, "for Endless is my name" (D&C 19:10). Without it we would remain fallen. Prayer becomes the vital lifeline, linking us to a complete understanding of our eternal potential as well as our utter dependence on Him.

The sooner the divine paradox is recognized and embraced, the more easily we "become as little children" (Matthew 18:3). We are more likely "to be entreated" (Alma 7:23) and are eager to be taught. We then wait upon the Lord, trusting that His timetable is better suited to our growth than is our myopic agenda. Without this patience, we might act with a toddler's timeline, pouting when there are delays and complaining incessantly. In pure paradox, our growing, childlike obedience becomes a sure sign of a more mature understanding.

Ultimately, our destiny includes receiving "all that [the] Father hath" (D&C 84:38). So great will be that blessing that "eye hath not seen, nor ear heard, neither have entered into the heart of man, the things which God hath prepared for them that love him" (1 Corinthians 2:9). But these only come to those who have declared their complete dependence—and patience—on the Eternal Father as well as on His timing.

4. Our God Is Not a Loophole God

A friend of mine once drove from Salt Lake City to St. George. Before leaving, he prayed that his car would function "from Salt Lake to St. George and back again." On returning, his car broke down just after they had crossed back into Salt Lake County. His conclusion? "I guess I should have prayed that we would make it all the way *home*, not just back to Salt Lake!"

While my friend saw humor in the whole situation (more than I might have had with a disabled car on the side of the road), he also highlighted a misconception many of us have about heavenly petitions: *The Father of our spirits is not looking for reasons to withhold blessings!* It is as if we think, as we might about an unethical business, that if He can "pay out" fewer blessings, He'll reduce His overhead "cost" and earn greater "profits"!

In fact, our God looks for reasons—any reasons—to bless us at the first opportunity. The history of the children of Israel, in Jerusalem and Zarahemla, is a testament to the great lengths the Lord will go to bless his people the minute they return to Him. Through forgetfulness and folly, sin and slumber, He pours down answers and blessings as quickly as it is in our best interest to do so. He asks only that we call frequently on His name and begin the process.

"They mount up to the heaven," the psalmist sings, "they go down again to the depths; their soul is melted because of trouble. They reel to and fro, and stagger like drunken man, and are at their wits end. *Then they cry unto the Lord in their trouble and he bringeth them out of their distresses.* He maketh the storm a calm, so that the waves thereof are still. Then are they glad because they be quiet; so he bringeth them unto their desired haven" (Psalm 107:26–30, emphasis added).

It is in His very eternal nature to want to bless His children. It would be contrary to Him to look for reasons and ways to arbitrarily withhold blessings we are in need of. One indictment sometimes made against God, generally by those with less understanding, is that God somehow "plays games" or "tests us" by deliberately ignoring our petitions.

In reality, most who have waited patiently will readily attest there was no game playing in the Lord's delay. Only in retrospect, can they finally see that the Lord took the requisite time to complete the entire tapestry rather than prematurely unfolding it to pleading and impatient eyes.

I once worked with a man who was emotionally devastated by the unexpected loss of his job. He struggled vainly for months to find work. Even more vainly, he struggled in prayer for answers and direction that didn't seem to be forthcoming. Over time he grew more despondent and depressed. Finally, after six months of fruitless searching, a new career path suddenly opened up for him. As it did, he saw the new job as an exact fit for his skills and interests. Later he discovered that his new company—the one he fit so perfectly with—had only recently moved into his state and would not have been available to him at the time he first lost his job. It was only then that he finally realized that there had been no needless delay; the Lord was simply preparing the right situation for him. The job opportunity was presented to him at the first possible opportunity.

In summary, we begin our search by taking stock of our prayers and of ourselves. We can be warmed by the wonderful things we know *for sure* about the Great God of the Universe. He is unchanging and consistent. He loves us and desires only the best for His children. He is anxious for us to pray and receive the answers prepared for us. And He will respond to those prayers as quickly as is good for us with the answers we need.

These things we know for sure. We know these things because prophets have taught them and continue to teach them. We also know them because our hearts tell us they are true, by the power of the Holy Ghost. They make sure we maintain our course despite the storm's wrath. So now that we've taken our celestial bearings, let us sail on!

Notes

1. J. Reuben Clark Jr., "Excerpts from *The Charted Course of the Church in Education*," *Ensign*, Sep. 2002, 54–61.
2. "Young Women Theme," *Young Women Personal Progress: Standing As a Witness of God* (booklet, 2001), 5.

chapter three

WE PRAY WITH OUR HEARTS

THE HEIGHTS BY GREAT MEN REACHED AND KEPT
WERE NOT ATTAINED BY SUDDEN FLIGHT,
BUT THEY, WHILE THEIR COMPANIONS SLEPT
WERE TOILING UPWARD IN THE NIGHT

LONGFELLOW

fter the death of Jacob, Lehi's descendants slowly slid into apostasy. They continued for about 300 years with very little spiritual light. The long night of darkness finally ended with Mosiah, father of King Benjamin. Warned by the Lord to leave their original land of inheritance, he took his people and joined with the people of Zarahemla, the Mulekites. After this migration, both he and Benjamin helped the two groups of people overcome years of generational apostasy. Mormon explains that King Benjamin was "a holy man and he did reign over his people in righteousness." The people were taught with "power and with authority . . . and much sharpness." Finally, after Benjamin's "laboring with the might of his body and the faculty of his whole soul" (Words of Mormon 1:17, 18), the people listened, and righteousness was restored.

Spiritual waxing and waning are constant subplots throughout the Book of Mormon. Repentance is always followed by great prosperity and then a rapid slide into wickedness. King Benjamin anxiously sought to prevent that. Near the end of his life, Benjamin called his people to a vast general conference at the temple to transfer the kingdom to his son Mosiah. At this historic meeting, he also planned to "give this people a name, that thereby they may be distinguished above all the people which the Lord God hath brought out of the land of Jerusalem; and this I do because *they have been a diligent people* in keeping the commandments of the Lord" (Mosiah 1:11, emphasis added).

It might rightly be asked what the people had left to accomplish. They had repented. They were "diligent" in keeping the commandments. Everything suggests they were living just as they should have been. What more could be expected?

We might ask the same question. We attend church and serve in callings. We helped the Jones move last Saturday—down three flights of stairs! We're not perfect, but we do the best we can. Isn't that enough? King Benjamin's answer to us might be the same as it was to his people—it's a good start! His classic address suggests that activity in the Church is just the beginning. As we keep the commandments and do what we're supposed to do, we are preparing for a wonderful, personal transformation. *And it is this transformation that changes our prayers and how we look to heaven for answers.*

King Benjamin began his address with a reminder of the selfless way he had governed his people. He had been their king, but he was also their servant. Using himself as an example, Benjamin taught them about their heavenly King. He wanted them to realize "the greatness of God and [their] own nothingness" (Mosiah 4:11). Despite their conversion and acts of righteousness, they were still "less than the dust of the earth" (Mosiah 4:2). The natural man—their natural selves—"is an enemy to God and will be, forever and ever, unless he yields to the enticings of the Holy Spirit, and . . . becometh as a child, submissive, meek, humble, patient, full of love, willing to submit to all things which the Lord seeth fit to inflict upon him" (Mosiah 3:19).

He then reminded them that the law of Moses did not have the power to save them. In addition, despite the fact there would one day be a judgment, their own obedience would not save them either. What they still lacked was a deep-seated fundamental change *in their hearts.* They needed to take upon them the name of Jesus Christ and allow Him to make the necessary change. They could not do it themselves. For this to occur, there would have to be a complete and total surrender of their wills to the great Mediator.

King Benjamin's address evoked the desired response in his people. He paused when he saw that his people had "fallen to the earth, for the fear of the Lord had come upon them" (Mosiah 4:1). They stated that they were desirous that they might be cleansed and their hearts purified. Their meekness and humility invited the promised changes in their hearts. That willingness was met with the desired response from the Holy Ghost. They exclaimed that "the Spirit of the Lord Omnipotent . . . has wrought a mighty change in us, or *in our hearts*" (Mosiah 5:2, emphasis added).

Their transformation stands as an example—and a reminder—to Saints in other ages as well. Activity and involvement in the Church organization does not automatically bring the heartfelt change King Benjamin spoke about. Personal righteousness teaches us obedience and prepares our hearts for the greater transformational changes to come.

It is critical to note that the change of heart received by Benjamin's followers was done *for them*, not *by them*. No matter how much they might have wanted a change to occur, they did not possess, of themselves, the power to make that change. Change of heart, like faith, hope, and charity, is a gift, bestowed on those who have placed themselves in a position to receive it.

President Marion G. Romney observed: "It would appear that membership in the Church and conversion are not necessarily synonymous. Being converted, as we are here using the term, and having a testimony are not necessarily the same . . . either. [Conversion comes] in stages until a person becomes 'at heart a new person.' "[1] The truthfulness of this fact is demonstrated by the large number of endowed Latter-day Saints who no longer hold current temple recommends.

Effective Prayers Begin in the Heart

The scriptures describe a wide variety of "heart conditions." There are "hard hearts" and "softened hearts," "broken hearts" and "contrite hearts." These might contrast with "proud hearts" and hearts "set on evil." But He who changes hearts declared, "I, the Lord, *require the hearts* of the children of men" (D&C 64:22).

For us to begin to comprehend what the Lord desires of us, we first need to clarify what a heart *is not*. A heart is neither a mind nor thoughts. The scriptures consistently separate minds from hearts. When Moroni asks us to ponder in our hearts (see Moroni 10:3), he is not suggesting a detailed analysis.

A "heart" is not simply a set of emotions. A young friend of mine, looking for reasons to distance himself from the rules of the Church, seized on a medical report that detailed the flow of blood through the brain during different emotional states. Different emotions were found to activate different parts of the brain. "See!" he exclaimed, "the Spirit is just neurons firing in the brain!" What he missed was the fact that we generally experience emotions *after* being filled with the Spirit. Our emotions are a reaction to the prompting, not the reason for it.

During the course of our lives, we are filled with a wide array of temporary emotions: anger or rage or love or fear. My own emotions act like the gauges in my car; they provide me with feedback on what is going on with me at any given moment. They also warn me when something is wrong that I need to pay attention to.

In truth, our hearts are our truest selves, the sources of our deepest yearnings. These innermost desires can be positive or negative, evil or righteous. Our daily decisions derive from trying to attain these desires. In addition, they determine our focus and goals, even those we may not be conscious of. What our heart is "set on" receives our best time and effort. Identify your true desires and you will understand what you love most.

It is this heart, this deepest level of commitment, that the Savior requires of us. When we truly desire these changes, the Holy Ghost can begin the needed transformation. When we are humble and teachable, these changes will be done to us, for us. As the Nephites correctly noted: "the Spirit of the Lord . . . *has wrought* a mighty change in us, *or in our hearts*" (Mosiah 5:2). A meek and childlike contrition seeks for these changes, gladly inviting the Spirit as a permanent companion. The result is that the Spirit of Jesus Christ "lives in us."

This wonderful transformation begins as hearts and lives are placed, without reserve, on the altar of God. Neal A. Maxwell eloquently observed, "the submission of one's will is placing on God's altar the only uniquely personal thing one has to place there."[2] At this point we become little children, ready to submit to anything and everything the Lord has for us. Recognizing our own "nothingness" is part of this process. "All that the father hath" is given to those who understand how little they can do on their own.

This was one of the important lessons Joseph Smith learned during his terrible ordeal in Liberty Jail. As he and the other brethren languished for months, they received reports of abuse and degradation being heaped on the Saints as they were being driven from the state in the middle of winter. The Prophet was powerless to provide any kind of help. In an effort to give a measure of comfort, he wrote a long letter to the Church in March of 1839. Parts of this letter later became sections 121, 122, and 123 of the Doctrine and Covenants.

From that letter comes this familiar plea,

> O God, where art thou? And where is the pavilion that covereth thy hiding place?
>
> How long shall thy hand be stayed, and thine eye, yea thy pure eye, behold from the eternal heavens the wrongs of thy people . . . ?" (D&C 121:1–2)

He then draws comfort from the Lord's answer, "My son, peace be unto thy soul; thine adversity and thine afflictions shall be but a small moment" (D&C 121:7).

What is not as well known is the portion of the letter that lies between the prophet's plea and the Lord's reply. Between the two is this lonely disclosure, recorded in the letter:

"Those who have not been enclosed in the walls of prison . . . can have but little idea how sweet the voice of a friend is . . . it seizes the present with avidity of lightening; it grasps the future with the fierceness of a tiger; it moves the mind backward and forward . . . until finally all enmity, malice and hatred . . . are slain victorious at the feet of hope; *and when the heart is sufficiently contrite, then the voice of inspiration steals along and whispers*—[my son, peace be unto thy soul . . .].[3]

Joseph was in Liberty Jail as a result of dark betrayals from those he considered his friends. He got constant reports of the stream of pain and abuse being heaped upon the Saints he loved. And yet, while in these most trying circumstances, Joseph learned that until his heart was right, revelation would be withheld. The Holy Ghost, testifying to the love of Christ, is not compatible with feelings of enmity, malice, or hatred, no matter how justified they may seem. Answers come to those whose hearts are contrite, tender, and open to heavenly guidance.

These monumental changes alter our relationship with our Heavenly Father. They draw us closer to Him and His desires. Hearts that are transformed desire the same things He desires. Those desires are His desires; His love our love. In this setting, our Church callings may remain the same, but our motivations change. Love replaces duty as desperation becomes inspiration.

Yet, while wading through our trials, we might argue that we are praying with "all our hearts." As we discussed in the last chapter, surrendered hearts are willing to follow any course the Lord directs. In truth, we may be praying with all our desires, but we are focused on getting exactly what we think we want when we want it.

Obedience to promptings, then, can become more critical than our immediate trials. Conversely, reluctance to let go of a treasured sin, for instance, is testimony that the transformation has not yet occurred. The Lord is unable to change hearts protected by a spiritual prenuptial agreement.

Early in my career as a psychotherapist, I received a call from a newly called bishop. Not long after being set apart, he discovered that his ward had some significant problems. Several ward members, serving in trusted positions, were guilty of serious transgressions. When he recognized both the severity and the extent of the problems, he moved forward with love and determination. Disciplinary courts were held, memberships were lost, and families threatened to be torn apart. It was a difficult time for everyone involved.

However, this loving bishop had a deep recognition for the exact needs of his flock. When he first called me, he explained his personal belief that the reason for the members' errant behavior was twofold: first, they had areas of their lives that required a serious examination. For this reason, they needed professional help (which was why he called me). He then explained that although these good people were all lifelong members of the Church, he believed that they simply did not understand the gospel or they wouldn't have committed the acts they did.

He understood, as did Alma, that "the preaching of the word had a . . . more powerful effect upon the minds of the people than the sword, or anything else, . . . therefore Alma thought it was expedient that they should try the virtue of the word of God" (Alma 31:5).

For these reasons, after each court action, the bishop also made an appointment for each errant brother or sister with a seasoned member of the ward who began a series of gospel discussions with them, reteaching the Atonement. Under this plan, the bishop generally reconvened their disciplinary courts less than a year later. While I helped these people change destructive habits, the Lord was changing their hearts.

"None of us," says Elder F. Enzio Busche, "has enough wisdom, enough intelligence, enough knowledge, enough skills, or enough courage, by ourselves, to master our lives and even to succeed in life unless we learn what it means to surrender ourselves into the arms of the Lord and be filled with the Spirit."[4]

As we look at the power of this transformation, we might ask, "How will I know when my heart is changed? The Apostle Paul gives us some sure indicators:

> Though I speak with the tongues of men and of angels, and have not charity, I am become as sounding brass, or a tinkling cymbal.
>
> And though I have the gift of prophecy, and understand all mysteries, and all knowledge; and though I have all faith, so that I could remove mountains, and have not charity, I am nothing.
>
> And though I bestow all my goods to feed the poor, and though I give my body to be burned, and have not charity, it profiteth me nothing.
>
> Charity suffereth long, and is kind; charity envieth not; charity vaunteth not itself, is not puffed up,
>
> Doth not behave itself unseemly, seeketh not her own, is not easily provoked, thinketh no evil;
>
> Rejoiceth not in iniquity, but rejoiceth in the truth;
>
> Beareth all things, believeth all things, hopeth all things, endureth all things.
>
> Charity never faileth: but whether there be prophecies, they shall fail; whether there be tongues, they shall cease; whether there be knowledge, it shall vanish away. (1 Corinthians 13:1–8)

Many read into Paul's discourse a need to be involved in charitable activities—volunteering at the local soup kitchen or extending meaningful service to a needy family in the ward. However, a closer examination of the list makes that interpretation an impossibly high standard to ever master. Despite our best efforts, there have been times when our charity *did* fail, when we didn't endure or hope like we needed to. But Elder Jeffrey R. Holland has pointed out that the above passage generally refers to a single source of charity, an unfailing type of divine love: the love of our Savior, Jesus Christ.

"*True charity has been known only once*. It is shown perfectly and purely in Christ's unfailing, ultimate, and atoning love for us. It is Christ's love for us that 'suffereth long, and is kind, and envieth not.' It is his love for us that is not 'puffed up . . . , not easily provoked, thinketh no evil.' *It is Christ's love for us that 'beareth all things, believeth all things, hopeth all things, endureth all things.'* "⁵

Perfect love flows from the Savior through us and outward to all we serve. We may occasionally fail, but the Lord and His love never do. We may become "puffed up" or "provoked," but Jesus Christ always sees past petty criticisms. *It is He that does not fail.* To be filled with that kind of love changes our nature and our behavior. It also helps us see that a marvelous transformation is well under way. And it will make sure that our prayers are never the same again.

In other words, the illuminating, warming spirit of love creates new creatures in Christ. His perfect love directs and teaches how to bless those we meet. How we love is then dictated by the perfect love from above. And it is that love that teaches us how to pray and receive answers to our prayers.

Surely, cry the skeptical, a lifetime of desires and habits change slowly, if at all. This conversion we talk about is difficult and complicated and requires people to make too many changes in all aspects of their lives. People will surely cling to their "comfort zone" and hesitate to venture outside. *You are asking way too much!*

The answer to all this hand wringing is that these monumental changes can occur as quickly as we desire them. This earth is not our original home. We lived long before this life. Our mortal history and experiences here represent the shortest period of time in our entire existence.

The "real me" descended from an existence filled with the love that flows from my Heavenly Father. Eternities were spent being submissive to Him, learning from Him, and desiring to be like Him. As my heart is changed, I am simply returning to my original, premortal state. Deep within, part of me recognizes just how this submission felt in that prior life. It was what I knew for countless millennia. It felt safe and secure and was filled with the joy that came from being obedient to the great plan of happiness. To have my heart changed would return me back to what I once knew. For me—for all of us—it is our best, most natural way to relate to the Father of our spirits.

To resist or delay this conversion is to continue to pray with the natural-man prayer we've talked about. Prayers of this sort are uttered, as the brother of Jared learned, only during times of trouble and quickly discontinued as soon as the trial has passed. They are directed to the

One we assume will solve our problem and rescue us from distress. *Fix the problem,* we plead, *just don't change me.* Again, the natural man also wants to dictate the terms of the deliverance, design the outcome and demand a timely response. Small wonder, then, that we soon become impatient or frustrated or depressed.

In conclusion, the Lord desires to change us into effective disciples, capable of and anxious to assist in serving His children. In order to do that, we need to have our earthly natures changed.

Notes

1. Marion G. Romney in Conference Report, Oct. 1963 (Salt Lake City: The Church of Jesus Christ of Latter-day Saints), 24.
2. Neal A. Maxwell, *If Thou Endure It Well* (Salt Lake City: Deseret Book, 2002), 54.
3. Joseph Fielding Smith, *Teachings of the Prophet Joseph Smith* (Salt Lake City: Deseret Book, 1967), 134.
4. F. Enzio Busche, "Unleashing the Dormant Spirit," BYU Devotional, May 14, 1996, 3.
5. Jeffrey R. Holland, *Christ and the New Covenant: The Messianic Message of the Book of Mormon* (Salt Lake City: Deseret Book, 1997), 336, emphasis by the author.

SPIRITUAL SUNBLOCK

> FORGIVENESS IS THE FRAGRANCE THAT A FLOWER LEAVES
> UPON THE HEEL THAT CRUSHES IT.
>
> UNKNOWN

*A*number of years ago, I spent several days learning how to sail. Determined to master this ancient art, I spent hour after hour gamely battling a small sailboat and an ever-shifting breeze. Each morning I was offered sunblock so that I wouldn't get burned by the sun reflecting off the water. Each time I turned it down, proudly explaining that I don't burn very easily and that I would be just fine. Two days later I paid dearly for my pride. The combination of the sun and the shimmering lake left me with a sunburn so severe I was ill for the next two days. At the same time, my friends who had wisely covered themselves with sunblock showed little sign of ever having been in the sun at all.

I have since marveled at how effective good sunblock can be. Two people can be exposed to the same sunlight, both feeling the same warmth. With sunblock in place, however, it is as if there were no sun because there is no lasting effect.

Spiritual experiences can be very similar. Many people can be in a meeting where the Spirit is present, powerfully testifying to the truthfulness of what is being said. Some in the meeting will be permanently affected, their hearts touched and new commitments made. They will later remember that meeting with fondness as a time when their testimonies were strengthened. Others, however, sitting in the same meeting, will describe feeling nothing and will be left unchanged by the exact same experience. It is as if they were wearing spiritual sunblock that prevented the Spirit from touching their skin or leaving a mark.

The Church long enjoyed the humble devotion and broad scholarship of the late Hugh Nibley. Brother Nibley was truly one of the greatest intellects the Church has ever produced. For him, all gospel scholarship was centered in the House of the Lord. In his autobiography he states: "If I went to the temple five times and nothing happened, I would stop going. But I've gone hundreds of times and the high hopes of new knowledge with which I go up the hill every week are never disappointed."[1]

One evening, while attending a session in the Provo Temple, I found Brother Nibley sitting a row ahead of me. I determined to watch how he responded to the presentation of the endowment and if he still appeared to be learning. His example that night forever changed the way I worship in the temple.

During the session, Brother Nibley listened intently to what was being said. Something in the presentation would appear to spark an intense, internal debate within, causing him to silently speak and visibly gesture to himself. From where I sat, I could clearly see that he had just learned something new and exciting. After a moment or two, he would again pause, listen, and then begin his animated but silent lecture to himself. As the session progressed, I became more and more jealous. I wanted to know what he was learning! Silently, great truths were being discovered and discussed. Despite all of Brother Nibley's vast knowledge, he was still plumbing the depths of the knowledge found only in the Lord's House. That night, I determined to pay more attention and to ask more questions about the endowment each time I attended.

The other great lesson I learned that night was from watching an older gentleman sitting next to Brother Nibley. As Brother Nibley sat enthralled with his discoveries, the other patron slept through most of the session. The contrast between the two men was pretty stark. Great lessons were being taught to an honest seeker of truth. And instead of joining Brother Nibley in the feast, his fellow patron was slumbering, awakening only to see if the session was over yet.

The Lord is eager to communicate with us. It is critical to our eternal salvation that we allow Him to "live in us" and thus change our heart. If we allow that, we begin to have the kind of heavenly communication—and answers—we seek. When it is not happening, we may need to first look at any spiritual sunblock we might be wearing, those spiritual barriers causing us to slumber when great knowledge and counsel is so available.

While speaking at BYU, Elder F. Enzio Busche observed: "In my humble understanding, it can be said that there are only two elements that separate us from the Holy Spirit; First, our lack of desire to repent [change of heart], Second, our lack of desire to forgive."[2]

As we know, sin separates us from the Holy Ghost. In order to sin, a Latter-day Saint first needs to ignore the gift of the Holy Ghost received at baptism. A conscious decision is made to bypass its gentle warnings and thus gratify the natural man. It is for this reason that Elder Bruce C. Hafen accurately calls sin an "act of independence,"[3] meaning that in order for us to commit it, we have to consciously choose to act outside the direction the Lord has given us.

Desire to Repent

In order to remove destructive spiritual sunblock, we must constantly avail ourselves of the blessings and growth of the repentance process. The steps of repentance have been endlessly taught within the Church, in every class from Primary on up. We know them as the six Rs:

Recognize we have sinned.
Feel **Remorse**
Resolve to not do it again
Relate the sin to the bishop if necessary
Make **Restitution** if necessary
Refrain from the sin in the future.

One bishop relates the experience of being stopped by a young woman in the lobby prior to sacrament meeting. Pulling him aside, she quickly explained that her and her boyfriend had engaged in some serious moral transgressions the night before. She then explained that she had now completed the Rs and just needed to confess to the bishop. She needed him to know so that she could then go into the meeting and take the sacrament. This good bishop, sensing just how little this young woman understood about repentance, suggested she refrain from taking the sacrament and that they meet immediately after the meeting.

Now while this may be an extreme case, it nevertheless highlights a potential problem. In an effort to teach repentance to generations of primary children, we have put a premium on learning the "steps to repentance," usually a series of R words. These are memorized and repeated at the beginning of each Sunday School lesson on repentance.

The problem lies not in the words on the list. Each is a necessary part of the repentance process. The difficulty is that there is one R word usually missing from most lists. While trying to memorize each step, we can unwittingly forget the most important R word of all: Redeemer!

This is not a small nor insignificant matter of semantics. Without total reliance on the Savior and His Atonement throughout every aspect of sincere repentance, we might have a tendency to believe that forgiveness was achieved on our own merits. We might believe that if *we* accomplished all the steps and *we* made the necessary amends, then *we* did it.

It is as if we had foolishly dug a large hole in our neighbor's garden and then simply spent a couple of minutes making it right. We cannot simply repair the hole in our spiritual life and return to our premortal innocence, no matter how long we take. One sin, any sin, and we are unworthy to return unless the Mediator makes up the difference.

Part of the difficulty comes in our view of how the Lord will judge us. When I was in school, for instance, I had a history teacher who would give exams and then post the test results on the board the next day. Grading on the dreaded "curve" he would write:

100
98   A
96

88
87   B
84

79
78   C
77

I always knew, as I looked at my grade in comparison to the rest of the class, that I could have gotten a higher grade if I had just a) studied harder, b) cheated, c) crammed, or d) turned in some type of large extra credit assignment at the last minute. I, along with others, also silently glared at the "curve busters" in the class. Their impossibly high scores had moved the rest of our scores down a notch.

Now, as most of us grew up with this kind of judgment, we may be tempted to see our eternal "grading" in the same way.

100		
98	A	*celestial*
96		
88		
87	B	*terrestrial*
84		
79		
78	C	*telestial*
77		

Looking around at others in church, we might see those who appear to be blessed more. Their kids are better behaved; they drive nicer cars; they're given callings of more responsibility. They seem, somehow, to be A Saints, those dreaded curve busters who make the rest of us look a little more shabby, a little less blessed. They appear to be setting an impossible standard for everyone else.

One client explained she was eternally worried that she would stand before the Lord on Judgment Day only to find she was a few "obedience points" short of the celestial kingdom. As a result, the Lord would smile and then send her away, cast off from the rest of her family. "I worry about that a lot," she confided, "but in my heart, that just doesn't feel right." I suggested she listen more closely to her heart and the truth she could feel within.

Here in the midterm of our lives, there doesn't seem to be anything we can do to bring our grades up—no cheating, cramming, or extra projects—before the final grades will be posted. If we're not careful, we might even be tempted to wonder if the Lord isn't a little selective, giving some people extra blessings or talents while leaving the rest of us to struggle as best we can.

If we catch ourselves with this kind of destructive thinking, it is important we remind ourselves of an important fact: *there is no curve at the final judgment.* "He employeth no servant there" (2 Nephi 9:41). All of us, no matter how talented or prosperous we may look, *will* be judged on our merits, *will* fall short, and *will* need One who can say, "Behold the sufferings . . . of him who did no sin. . . . Wherefore, Father, spare these my brethren" (D&C 45:4–5). Entrance into the kingdom of heaven will require us to have done all we can and then depend on His tender mercies to give us what we clearly did not earn or deserve.

It was the prophet Nephi who proclaimed, "We talk of Christ, we rejoice in Christ, we preach of Christ, we prophesy of Christ . . . that our children may know to what source they may look *for a remission of their sins*" (2 Nephi 25:26, emphasis added).

A few years ago I worked with an older man who struggled with a terrible self-image. Years before, he had carried on an extramarital affair with a sister in his ward. Many in the ward came to know about the affair, and it was some time before he finally went to the bishop and confessed. Excommunication soon followed.

Some ten years after he had been rebaptized, he still had never attempted to have his temple blessings restored. He floated between wards, always sitting near the back of the meetings. When asked why, his explanation was painfully simple: "I am an adulterer and don't deserve to serve in any callings. Most people in the ward know what I did, and I'm sure they don't want to be around me." What he would neglect to say was that he was always the first to volunteer for service projects and would help anyone in the ward as soon as he was asked. Faithfully attending his meetings, he spent long years viewing himself on the outside of Church fellowship. Prayers were a burden because he believed God continued to see him only as "the adulterer."

This church has many good-hearted Saints, like this good brother, who have made mistakes in their lives and do not yet understand the freeing power of the Atonement. They silently mop the floors of the church community, carrying the guilt and pain of past sins. They compare themselves with others at church, constantly selling themselves short. In their eyes, they are eternal second-class Saints, grateful to merely gather the crumbs left by more worthy Church members.

On the other hand, newly repentant hearts, who come to fully understand the Atonement, are close to the Spirit. They glisten with gratitude for the mercy of the Savior. Their meekness and softened hearts are especially open to promptings and heavenly directions. The Spirit is able to teach them new truths, providing them with the answers they always sought but could not find.

Another type of repentance is the kind begun by the Lord. Some fear to turn to the Lord because, like the brother of Jared, there may be a rebuke waiting for them at the top of the mountain. Opening the heart to the Spirit invites the Lord in. As He enters, He may remind us of things we neglected. "As many as I love," the Lord reminded John on the isle of Patmos, "I rebuke and chasten" (Revelations 3:19). Joseph Smith was similarly told that "ye must needs be chastened and stand rebuked before my face" (D&C 95:2).

How we handle chastisement tells us a great deal about the condition of our hearts and how anxious we are to find the answers we seek. If we cannot take the Lord's rebuke, or even a priesthood leader's, we may decide that the price of our answers is too high. We forget, as we cling to the vestiges of our tattered pride, that "with the chastisement I prepare a way for their deliverance in all things out of temptations, *and I have loved you*" (D&C 95:1, emphasis added).

One client had struggled with pornography for years. It ate away at his relationship with his wife and family, but he managed to keep it a secret for almost twenty years. Then one night, his wife returned home earlier than he expected and caught him in the act. This led to painful arguments, tearful visits with their bishop, and an appointment with me. As the months passed and he continued to heal, he spoke with excitement of the increased emotional intimacy between him and his wife. She confirmed the new strength present between them. Eventually, the Lord responded to his humility and helped remove the cravings. In retrospect, having his addiction discovered and challenged helped change his marriage—but only as he was willing to humble himself and repent.

Heavenly Father sometimes chastises His children to help them change. The only motive He has is to help them become what He desires that they become. This is far different than the scolding that comes from someone who has been inconvenienced or embarrassed. Divine chastisement results in a call to change—to improve—and a chance to feel the Savior's love.

A great example of inspired correction is contained in the life of Parley P. Pratt. Elder Pratt served the Church and the Lord from the moment he knew the Book of Mormon was true to the day he was murdered. But even Parley had to be occasionally corrected. Perhaps the most well-known example occurred as he led a group of pioneers toward the Salt Lake Valley. Before leaving Winter Quarters, Brigham Young had made promises to the members of the Mormon Battalion that their families would be cared for and brought to the valley. Elder Pratt, leading a separate pioneer company, had forged ahead with the strongest and most well-prepared families, leaving the others to wait. Many of those left behind were families of the "Battalion boys."

When Brigham Young was returning to Winter Quarters from the valley, he met Elder Pratt's company out on the trail. President Young soon discovered that many of battalion families had been left behind. Parley himself described Brigham's reaction:

> A council was called, in which I was highly censured and chastened by President Young and others. . . . In short, I was severely reproved and chastened. *I no doubt deserved this chastisement*; and I humbled myself, acknowledged my faults and errors, and asked forgiveness. I was frankly forgiven, and, bidding each other farewell, each company passed on their way. This school of experience made me more humble and careful in future, and I think it was the means of making me a wiser and better man ever after.[4]

The measure of Elder Pratt's spiritual greatness, I believe, is readily apparent in the way he handled a painful and potentially embarrassing situation. He could have been highly defensive, defending his actions by explaining he had done the best he knew how to do under trying circumstances. Instead, he humbled himself, took the correction, received inspired counsel from his priesthood leaders, and then moved on.

Desire to Forgive

Let's now look at the second part of Elder Busche's statement: "In my humble understanding, it can be said that there are only two elements that separate us from the Holy Spirit; First, our lack of desire to repent, *Second, our lack of desire to forgive*."

Contained in the Savior's Sermon on the Mount is this daunting statement, "forgive us our debts as we forgive our debtors" (Matthew

6:12). Said another way, "Lord, forgive all my sins, no matter how great or small, as quickly and completely as I forgive those who have hurt me." In one simple statement, the Savior of the world tied our forgiveness and our salvation not just on the way we treat others, but also on how we feel about them—regardless of what they might have done to us.

I have a friend who had been consistently abused by her father from a very early age. Her early experience colored her life in a wide variety of ways. She struggled with depression and self-esteem problems. She had great difficulty with friendships. The greatest burden she carried was a belief, common to many victims of abuse, that she had somehow caused the abuse to occur—that it was her fault.

Somewhere in her recovery, she met a friend who was a member of the Church. She liked what she heard and felt the difference when she was around members of the Church. Soon afterward she was baptized. A year later, she asked if I would be willing to be in attendance when she went to the temple for the first time. As we stood together in the lobby, she looked around nervously and whispered, "I'm waiting for the walls to fall in on me."

"Why?" I asked.

"Because the Lord will find out I'm here," she said.

"Are you afraid you're not worthy?"

She nodded.

"Did your bishop give you a recommend?"

"Yes."

"Did you answer truthfully?"

"Of course!"

"Did he pronounce you worthy to enter the temple?"

"That's what he said."

"Then," I said, "the problem is that you don't believe your bishop."

"That's right," she said, "I still feel guilty."

It took another few years for her to finally rid herself of the sense that she was responsible for her father's abuse when she was a child. To her credit, she has forgiven him, but she still deals with bad relationships and poor decision making. That forgiveness was not easy, nor did it come quickly. Only when she recognized what a destructive life he had lived and how little insight he would ever have into his problems was she able to forgive him. It did not mean she needed to maintain a close relationship with him—he was still abusive and toxic to be around—but she could let it go and move on with her life.

Forgiving those who have "trespassed against us" may be the most Christlike behavior we can perform in this life—and possibly the most difficult. To be genuine, our heart must let go of the bitterness, anger, and resentment that cankers our soul and robs us of the spiritual peace we desire. This cankering may stand as sunblock between us and the spiritual promptings we seek.

We can be comforted, though, by the assurance that One who knows exactly how to forgive will be our guide in the process. In other words, to communicate with our Heavenly Father, we must learn to forgive like the Son, who meekly knelt in the garden and bore the unfair weight of sins He did not commit.

Finally, one additional spiritual sunblock that can come between us and the spirit of the Lord is pride. This original sin clouds our soul and blocks heavenly communication. Hearts puffed up with pride pray only to "consume it upon their lusts." Pride distorts our requests and leaves us with hearts so focused on our own myopic view of life as to obscure any heavenly responses.

"Pride gets no pleasure out of having something," warns C. S. Lewis, "only out of having more of it than the next man. We say that people are proud of being rich, or clever, or good-looking, but they are not. *They are proud of being richer, or cleverer, or better-looking than others.* If everyone else became equally rich, or clever, or good-looking there would be nothing to be proud about. It is the comparison that makes you proud: the pleasure of being above the rest. Once the element of competition has gone, pride has gone."[5]

I believe that in our spiritual growth, the time will come when we will have to choose between our pride and the answers we desire. We cannot have both. Heavenly Father will not give us answers for us to "consume it upon our lust," nor will a prideful heart willingly accept answers contrary to what it demands. The good news is that pride cannot stand up under the withering warmth of the Spirit. As we draw on the Redeemer's love for our repentance and extend that love to those who have hurt us, we will find pride melting away like an icicle on a sunny day.

Notes

1. Hugh Nibley, "An Intellectual Autobiography," *Nibley on the Timely and the Timeless* (Provo, Utah: BYU Religious Studies Center, 1978), xxviii.

2. F. Enzio Busche, "Unleashing the Dormant Spirit," BYU Devotional, May 14, 1996, 6.
3. Bruce C. Hafen, *Applying the Atonement to Life's Experiences* (Salt Lake City: Deseret Book, 1978), 39.
4. *Autobiography of Parley P. Pratt* (Salt Lake City: Deseret Book, 1985), 330–31.
5. C. S. Lewis, *Mere Christianity* (London: Collier, 1960), 109, emphasis added.

chapter five

STUPORS, FASTING, AND COVENANTS

A young father painfully explains some serious medical issues his family is facing. He wonders aloud how he will pay for all the procedures his family will need. He also wonders if he should be finding another job or seeking other ways to meet this unexpected crisis. In attempting to understand better what he needs to do, he prays frequently but grows frustrated when no answers seem to be forthcoming.

His description is interesting. "I feel," he explained softly, "that praying is sometimes like going to the ATM machine but not being able to figure out the right PIN. I know there is money in there, but I just don't seem to have the right code. Am I supposed to fast or not? Pray all night or pray all the time? Plead or 'wait on the Lord'? And what, exactly, is a stupor?"

My young friend describes a feeling many of us have when we can't seem to get the promptings we need. We worry there is some magic formula we're missing. Have we offended God in some way we don't yet know?

In discussions with Latter-day Saints about this topic, two major questions inevitably arise: what are stupors and burnings, and what role does fasting play in getting answers? Let's take a look at these questions one at a time.

Stupors and Burnings

When I was a young missionary in England, my mission used a wonderful tool for teaching the gospel. We called it the fifteen-minute spiritual experience. While tracting, we would ask for just fifteen minutes of someone's time. When they agreed, we would come in and start with a word of prayer. Then we would have them read D&C 9:8, "But, behold, I say unto you, that you must study it out in your mind; then you must ask me if it be right, and if it is right I will cause that your bosom shall burn within you; therefore, you shall feel that it is right."

We would next explain that this was how the Holy Ghost worked. Next we would recite for them Joseph Smith's First Vision in his own words. Finally, we would bear our testimonies and leave. This approach proved very successful in having people invite us back. They often described having felt peaceful and calm.

Elder Mark E. Peterson of the Quorum of the Twelve was touring our mission at this time, and we had an opportunity to role play this approach with him, with him playing the part of the investigator. He listened attentively to the approach. Afterwards he said:

"Elders, this is a great approach and very well done. The only problem with it is that you're using wrong scriptures."

When asked what he meant, he went on to explain: "This section, talking about the burning in the bosom and the stupor of thought, was meant for Oliver Cowdery in the process of the translation of the Book of Mormon. It was not meant for the members of the Church generally."

He went on to expound that, while some feel the burning in the bosom and that might be their particular gift, he warned that we needed to be very careful in trying to generalize one particular manifestation of the Holy Ghost to everyone.

In response to his suggestions, we modified the scriptures we were using in our proselyting activities. His inspired counsel also gives us an important guideline in our prayerful communication with God. I have talked with many who have struggled mightily, trying to understand exactly what a stupor was or wasn't or why they hadn't gotten a burning response to their prayers.

What many of us forget is that we have all been blessed with various spiritual gifts. The Lord appears to have scattered those gifts among individuals in order for them to rely more on one another. Each gift is different. As a result, the way the Spirit works with us has been individualized.

I told the young father who was searching for the right "PIN" that many of us have felt the same way: needing answers, not getting them, and wondering if the fault were with us or our prayer methods, or if the Lord were withholding answers for a purpose. The result can be that we fear there is something wrong with our standing with God, in addition to the fact that we still don't have our needed answers!

Again, there are those for whom the confirmation/burning approach works on a regular basis. They can testify to its effectiveness in their lives. It is their gift. However, if this is not your gift—and for most of us it is not—then coming to understand your particular spiritual gift is part of gaining spiritual maturity.

Fasting

Nearly every Saint seeking heavenly answers has, at one time or another, considered the role fasting may play in the search for guidance. During these times of struggle, we become aware, for instance, of the experience the Savior had when He saw a group of disciples being verbally accosted by a large group of scribes. When the Savior asked the cause of the disagreement, a desperate father stepped forward to explain that he had brought his son to the disciples, hoping to have them cast out the demons that had wracked his son's body for many years. To the chagrin of the father, as well as the disciples, they were unsuccessful in casting out the evil spirits. Their very public failure had brought down the ridicule of the local scribes, who were celebrating. The Savior then healed the boy, casting out the demons that had caused the boy so much suffering.

Afterwards, the disciples, perhaps still smarting at their embarrassment, approached the Savior and asked, "Why could not we cast him out?" In response, the Lord teaches them that "this kind can come forth by nothing, but by prayer and fasting" (Mark 9:28, 29). This scripture is one we often use to tie prayer together with fasting, leaving us to wonder when and how we are supposed to fast when petitioning the Lord on certain matters.

If we are not careful, however, we can turn to fasting as the "last resort" or "extra project," the method used when we still aren't getting the answers we really want. When we use fasting in this manner, the logic can be somewhat confusing. It is as if we are saying that since we're not getting answers through "regular" or "normal" prayer, perhaps we need to fast to bulk up our attempts.

In actuality, it may be that we sometimes misunderstand the purpose and power of the law of the fast. In Doctrine and Covenants 59 the Lord explains:

> And on this day thou shalt do none other thing, only let thy food be prepared with singleness of heart that thy fasting may be perfect, or, in other words, that thy joy may be full.
>
> Verily, this is fasting and prayer, or in other words, *rejoicing and prayer*. (D&C 59:13–14, emphasis added)

The Lord is explaining to us that fasting and prayer is better described as rejoicing and prayer—that fasting is meant to be rejoicing. That is a powerful concept. The Savior, in trying to teach his struggling disciples, could just as easily have told them: "this kind can come forth by nothing, but by prayer and rejoicing."

Utilizing the priesthood of God in blessing the lives of God's children is meant to be a joyful experience, as is seeking answers from God. If fasting is used as an outward manifestation of our humility and submission, it can indeed be an aid when we are listening for, and then submitting to, the Lord's counsel.

For years, I found myself less than enthusiastic about fast Sunday. Not completely understanding this concept, I found it to be the slowest of the four Sundays every month! We would ask, on Sunday morning, "So what are we fasting for this time?" as though we were submitting our Christmas gift list. *Hmmm, what is it I want?*

However, in coming to understand the critical role of rejoicing—celebrating, if you will—I now enjoy "Gratitude Sunday" on the first Sunday of every month, happily refraining from eating as part of my gratitude and thankfulness for all I've been blessed with.

Can fasting play a role in gaining answers to prayers? Of course. It helps us focus, express our thankfulness, and put our hearts in the right submissive attitude to receive God's counsel to us. But we should be careful in organizing family or ward fasts to "fast and pray for Aunt Tilly to get well" unless we are inspired by the Holy Ghost that we are supposed to be fasting for that exact purpose. Otherwise, we might elect to gather in fasting and prayer that the Lord's will be done for Aunt Tilly and that we'll be inspired to understand what is to happen and what we can do to help. If her Heavenly Father has appointed her unto death, we might look a little foolish trying to convince the Lord that we know better than He does.

Again, as we are learning to gain answers to prayer and striving to better understand the spiritual mechanism that will bring us needed relief, we always need to return to the simple concept of praying to a God who knows more than we do, who loves us more than we love ourselves, and who knows better what it is we need and when we need it. We can become easily sidetracked trying to understand stupors or determining the length or type of fast required. As a result, in our desperation, we can make prayer much more complicated than it was intended to be—that is, the process of receiving answers from the Divine Source.

President Henry B. Eyring describes a time when he was attempting to make a major change in the Church Education System. He worried about the change being appropriate and being exactly what the Lord wanted. He describes pleading to know what to do but feeling nothing. Finally, after a lengthy struggle, he explains: "Somewhat to my surprise, I found myself praying, "Heavenly Father, it doesn't matter what I want. I don't care anymore what I want. *I only want that Thy will be done.* That is all that I want. Please tell me what to do."[1] His heartfelt struggle brought him to a point where he simply sought for what the Lord wanted. That complete meekness resulted in inspiration that ultimately blessed the lives of young adults around the world.

As we've discussed in earlier chapters, complete submission, that childlike willingness to "only want that Thy will be done" not only brings answers from heaven but also comforts us when it is not yet time for us to know what the Lord intends for us.

You Do Not Know How to Pray

The Prophet Joseph Smith also had a dilemma. Year by year, he continued to gain a greater knowledge as more was revealed to him. The increased light must have filled his soul with wonder. But with whom could he share it? How much knowledge could the Saints handle, especially the new converts? He desperately wanted them to progress and learn, but he also knew that increased light brings increased responsibility. He could not drown them in sacred knowledge they were spiritually unprepared for. At one point he exclaimed, "There has been a great difficulty in getting anything into the heads of this generation. It has been like splitting hemlock knots with a corn-dodger for a wedge and a pumpkin for a beetle!"[2] (In other words: It's like splitting hardwood knotholes using a pancake for a wedge and a pumpkin for the hammer.)

This was especially true as he worked to prepare the Saints for the blessings of the temple. Gospel knowledge was growing but still very fragile. The Saints needed to spiritually mature in many ways. Nothing in their former church traditions prepared them to know what to expect. Yet, temple blessings were needed, and Joseph's time was running out. To assist in their preparation, he held a series of classes and lectures, trying to prepare the Saints as best he could in the short time he had left.

One particular day, while taking some members through the construction site of the Nauvoo temple, the Prophet turned to Sister Bathsheba Smith and said, "you do not know how to pray or to have your prayers answered."[3] She took this to mean she would learn how to pray as part of her temple experience. And she was right.

Some might consider that comment a curious or even bold statement. Didn't the Savior, at the Sermon on the Mount, teach his disciples how to pray? And prayer is an essential element of most other religions and denominations. In addition, as Latter-day Saints we do not claim an exclusive on prayers or on receiving answers from a loving God, who is "no respecter of persons" (Acts 10:34). Aren't others entitled to receive answers to their prayers, despite never having entered an LDS temple?

True enough. But the Prophet taught that there is a pattern of divine prayer, learned in the temple, that provides a divine template to follow. The more we come to understand that template and extend it to our everyday prayers, the more we will discover a more intimate and instructive form of prayer. And, as we follow it, I believe we will endorse the Prophet's statement and admit we really didn't know how to pray!

There are three main elements of the divine pattern given in the temple:

1. Covenant making is an essential part of prayer.
2. If we are prepared, we are taught what to say.
3. Pure hearts combine with perfect unity to draw upon the powers of heaven.

Let's look at these three individually.

1. Covenant Making Is an Essential Part of Prayer

Every meeting in the Church, including the infamous church basketball game, begins with prayer—except for the temple. In that setting, we make sacred covenants, receive the promise of eternal blessings, and then, after having received almost two hours of instruction, we approach the Lord in prayer.

One of the reasons we pray in the first place is because of our belief in God's promises to hear and answer our prayers. He declared He would hear our prayers, and He does. When He covenants with mankind, He fulfills those covenants. His words are all fulfilled. We, on the other hand, make countless promises to Him, fail, and then plead for His forgiveness as we try again. Thankfully, His mercy allows us to take the sacrament each week, spiritually dust ourselves off, and try again.

What we should be praying for, in large measure, is help completing our covenants.

Praying with a face toward sacred places is a fixture for Jews and Muslims all over the world. These children of Abraham continue a long tradition of praying toward Jerusalem or Mecca as a way of reminding themselves of their responsibilities. I find that my own prayers take on an added dimension when, as I kneel by my bed, I turn to face the temple. Pictures of the covenants I have made there pass through my mind. Then, as I pray, I begin with gratitude for the promised blessings that await me if I simply follow through on what I've promised to do.

When we keep the covenants we've made, we approach the Lord with a greater level of confidence. It is not a feeling of entitlement, but rather a quiet assurance that He will sanctify our continuing efforts to serve in His kingdom. We feel the Spirit confirming that the Lord has beheld our sacrifice and will bless us in going forward. This assurance is expressed by a softened heart and a contrite spirit, the result of humble covenant keeping. It is accompanied by sincere gratitude for the changes these covenants make in our daily lives.

In our prayers we will then hear ourselves pleading for help to continue in the covenants we've promised to keep. As we do so, we make additional covenants. This happens because, as we're about to discuss, the Spirit leads us to make the kind of promises that bind us even more closely to our Heavenly Benefactor. Conversely, when we've been keeping covenants but not receiving needed answers, we can be more confident in those assurances that the Lord does keep His promises.

2. If We Are Prepared, We Are Taught What to Say

In chapter one, we talked about the importance of letting the Holy Ghost teach us what to say. Not long ago I was asked to speak to a priest and laurel conference in a rural area. I, like their inspired leaders, was very aware that many of these kids were the only LDS youth in their high school. These annual conferences had become a vital part of their lifeline to other youth with their same values and goals. In addition, many were about to graduate from high school and faced difficult decisions about their schooling, missions, and life in general. As I thought about my upcoming classes, I was prayerful that my remarks would be inspired and appropriate, given the challenges they faced. With those goals and their needs in mind, I prepared lessons I felt would meet their needs.

On the morning of the conference, I awoke with a start and felt a need to take a walk. After I had walked for the better part of an hour, I knew exactly what I was to say and how I was to say it. I hurried back and rewrote a lot of what I'd planned. During the classes that day, I felt the gentle power of the Spirit teaching these youth the things the Lord wanted them to know. While I was teaching, I listened almost as an observer at the truths being taught. Many times I would have liked to stop and quickly write down what I heard myself saying. Often the instruction was different than I would have given.

One of the marvelous aspects of the gospel of Jesus Christ is that what I have just described is not an unusual occurrence in this Church. Many of us have had similar experiences. Whether teaching a class, speaking in sacrament meeting, or talking to a nonmember, the Spirit takes over, *and we hear ourselves say things we hadn't planned on.* At those moments we are quickly reminded that this is His church, that we are talking to His children, and that we are simply the messenger chosen to provide the message.

On the other hand, most of us have also had the discouraging experience of assuming we knew what needed to be taught. Despite the whisperings of the Spirit to change or modify a lesson or talk, we push boldly forward with our thoughts because we've spent a lot of preparation time and we know (*we* know), what needs to be said. The result is pure misery—for us and for our listeners. We quickly discover just how inadequate we are without the Spirit and how empty our wonderful, prepared words are when stripped of inspiration.

In Romans 8, Paul tries to explain that *our prayers can be and should be the same way.* We do not always know what we should pray for. We think we know. We think we understand our needs. But if we allow the Spirit to "make intercession" for us (see Romans 8:26), we will learn that our real needs are those things the Lord knows we need.

Relationship experts have long suggested that love is a verb, meaning that we feel love when it is being generated by one who loves us. We also feel love as we generate love toward someone else. There is no love battery or a love stockpile that is tapped into when needed. It is there *as* we love someone or *as* they are loving us. That's why it's a verb, not a noun. It is a present feeling, regardless of whether we are the giver or the receiver.

Not long ago a tearful mother asked if I would visit with her inactive daughter. As I did so, I found the daughter to be bright and intelligent. However, she had left the Church right after high school and had broken about every commandment since then. One night, she confessed that a recently returned missionary had told her that, because of her disobedience, she would never be able to be with her family in the celestial kingdom. I listened to her and then told her of the great error she'd been told. This prompted a wonderful discussion about repentance and the power of the Atonement. As we talked, a sweet spirit filled the room. I pointed that spirit out to her and then explained, "Love is a verb. What you are now feeling is the Lord's spirit and, because of that, the Lord's love. He is loving you right now—in real time—at this moment. And He wants you to come home." Her response was interesting: "No one has ever explained that to me." When I asked her what she felt, she recognized the Spirit and confessed, "Wow. I haven't felt that in a long time." Shortly after that, she moved back home with a family that loves her.

There is a powerful lesson here when we apply this same principle to our relationship with our Heavenly Father. His love toward His children is active and current. We feel it because He is extending it toward us constantly. We feel His love because He is, at that very moment, loving us and caring about our situation. We feel it in real time, at the same moment He is feeling it toward us. If we can catch the full import of this principle, we can know the reality of our Heavenly Father on a daily basis.

In addition, when we feel His love and are filled with His spirit, we also hear His voice to us. "Verily, I say unto you, my friends," the Saints were told in 1832,

>I leave these sayings with you to ponder in your hearts, with this commandment . . . that ye shall call upon me while I am near—
>
>Draw near unto me and I will draw near unto you . . .
>
>Behold, that which you hear is as the voice of one crying in the wilderness—in the wilderness, because you cannot see him—*my voice, because my voice is Spirit* . . . and if it be in you it shall abound." (D&C 88:62–63, 66, emphasis added)

Have you felt His spirit? Then you have heard His voice! If you have heard His voice it was because He was near. And if you have felt His love it is because He is, at that very moment, loving you. It is also comforting to know that the love you feel is also felt, and certainly appreciated, in the heavenly courts above.

Consistently, my most wonderful experiences with prayer have occurred when I have allowed the Spirit I felt to take over my words and express the deepest aspects of my heart and soul. My words flow smoothly and beautifully. I hear eternal truths being expressed, and the language is far different. In looking back at those times, I have never felt more loved than I do at the moment the prayer is being uttered. No one is capable of loving with the intensity and mercy that He does.

Conversely, when I stubbornly stick to my prayer wish list, fearful that I might leave something or someone out, my prayers become more hit and miss. I have a difficult time picturing a Heavenly Father who says, "Well, I was going to bless Aunt Mable, but because Kevin neglected to mention her in his prayer, she's now on her own! Too bad he left her out."

3. Pure Hearts Combine with Perfect Unity to Draw upon the Powers of Heaven

There is an oft-repeated story of an incident that occurred during the translation of the Book of Mormon. As he began a morning of translation, Joseph found he could not translate. He realized he and Emma had disagreed about something and had parted with unresolved feelings still hanging in the air. This seemingly small distraction brought the process of revelation to a quick stop. He quickly realized there would be no translation until his feelings with Emma were resolved. He excused himself, sought forgiveness from Emma, and then returned and resumed the translation. The Spirit had been restrained until he had made the necessary peace.

Sometimes our disagreements are not with other people, they are more within us. The righteous desires of our hearts can be clouded or even mocked by our natural man or woman. This battle between head and heart can be fierce and destructive. And it destroys the relationships around us.

In trying to find creative ways to help people change, I used to take groups to a high adventure ropes course. This outdoor experience was a series of events and activities, some as a group, some individually, where therapeutic issues could be examined in a physical way. Perhaps the most dramatic and effective event was "the perch," which involved placing an individual into a safety harness attached to a belay rope. He or she would then climb a tree to a point forty feet above the ground and step onto a small platform. Because of the feeling of risk and fear, I found most people much more honest with their feelings while in that position. The therapy session was conducted by yelling back and forth between the ground and the tree.

During one session, the father of a large family took his place high up on the small perch. As he stood there trembling, he explained how miserable he was on a daily basis. In return, his wife, who stood next to me on the ground, shouted up to him that his misery was partly as a result of his need to always be in control. As he clung to the tree, he agreed with her, highlighted by just how out of control he felt at that moment. This experience was truly a mirror of his life, he realized, always wanting to be in control but never being able to control all the things in his life. The result was daily misery.

As he continued to gain insight into the source of his pain, I shouted up to him, "Mike, I think I understand you better. I believe you would rather be right than happy!" With that he started to laugh. His commitment, before he came down, was to allow himself more happiness and quit listening to the messages in his head telling him he always had to be in charge.

This is why King Benjamin explained that we need to "cast off" the natural man "and become as a little child." Why a child? What is there about a child that could counteract the worldly tantrums of the flesh? King Benjamin gives a partial answer, as we have discussed before. We become like a child when we are "submissive, meek, humble, patient, full of love, willing to submit to all things which the Lord seeth fit to inflict up on him" (Mosiah 3:19).

The more we become as little children, the more we can unite with others in friendship and love. That unity, which comes from a purified heart, enables us to form lasting friendships that build and strengthen our covenants. True joy, eternal joy, comes from these relationships.

There remains a last question here, one we frequently miss. Why would an adult choose the hollow companionships of the great and spacious building over the brotherhood of children of Zion? If we have felt the love of the Lord and the fellowship of the Saints, why would we settle for neon lights and the phony façade? Could it be that those who have known both do not feel worthy of Zion's loving embrace? Far too often that is exactly the reason. We are scrubbing floors when we should be dining at the feast.

And there is the glorious, staggering, eternal truth. When we cast off the natural man and become new creatures in Christ, we are cleansed by the blood of the Lamb. We become a new person with a new heritage—sons and daughters of Christ. We are born again.

To become like a child, we literally have to become innocent children again—as clean and pure as the day we entered this earth "in our infant state." Not only do we approach the Lord with more confidence, we also more easily join with others seeking to do the same thing. The pure in heart are pure in motive. This does not mean perfect, for they will not be perfect in this life. But their motives, driven by a heartfelt desire to become pure, lead them to surround themselves with the "elect." Devoid of conflict, prayer can become what the Lord intended it to be—divine desires from a pure heart.

Notes

1. Henry B. Eyring, "As a Child," *Ensign*, May 2006, 14–17, emphasis added.
2. Joseph Smith, *History of The Church of Jesus Christ of Latter-day Saints*, ed. B. H. Roberts (Salt Lake City: Deseret News, 1980), 6:184–85.
3. Truman G. Madsen, *Joseph Smith the Prophet* (Salt Lake City: Deseret Book, 2008), 98.

chapter six

PROMPTINGS OR ME?

THE VALUE OF CONSISTENT PRAYER IS NOT THAT HE WILL HEAR
US, BUT THAT WE WILL HEAR HIM.

WILLIAM MCGILL

During the cold winter of 1846–47, Brigham Young pre-pared as best he could for the upcoming trek to find a home for the Saints. His people were freezing, starving, and dying in places like Winter Quarters and Mt. Pisgah. Supplies—and morale—were running low. The Camp of Israel stood on the edge of disaster. President Young, as President of the Twelve, desperately needed answers for any one of a hundred decisions that needed to be made if the Church was going to survive to the following year.

In addition, some Saints who had crossed the icy Mississippi in February, waded through rain and mud in March, and fought disease through the summer, were growing restless and were now prime targets for splinter groups like James Strange's and Sidney Rigdon's. It seemed that all the forces of evil and weather had combined to destroy them before they could find refuge and a home.

Fortunately, the needed answers came, as they always do. One source of great comfort was the personal visits of the Prophet Joseph Smith to several of the brethren. Brigham and others were taught many things by the Prophet, who returned from the spirit world and provided much-needed counsel and spiritual support. Brigham explained that

Joseph had, on one occasion, said:

> Tell the people to be humble and faithful, and be sure to keep
> the spirit of the Lord and it will lead them right. Be careful and not
> turn away the small still voice; *it will teach you what to do and where
> to go*; it will yield the fruits of the kingdom. Tell the brethren to keep
> their hearts open to conviction, so that when the Holy Ghost comes
> to them, their hearts will be ready to receive it. *They can tell the Spirit
> of the Lord from all other spirits; it will whisper peace and joy to their
> souls*; . . . Tell the brethren if they will follow the spirit of the Lord
> they will go right. Be sure to tell the people to keep the Spirit of the
> Lord.[1]

Joseph's counsel from beyond the veil was a reminder to the struggling Saints that they would be able to understand the source of their
promptings. They would know divine counsel from "all other spirits" by
the degree of peace and joy it brought, along with taking away "malice,
hatred, strife and evil from their hearts."[2]

Like Brigham and those early Saints, we too have a constant need
for guidance and direction. At times, our testimony or our resolve may
stand on the edge. We need answers and reassurances to help us move
forward. Understanding the source of our spiritual responses will be
the key, for God's guidance is always communicated by the power of
the Holy Ghost, who "teacheth the peaceable things of the kingdom"
(D&C 36:2).

True, sometimes separating the promptings of the Spirit from the
pressures of our own thoughts and desires can be a delicate task. We
may feel we've experienced answers in response to our questions, but
then we pause while we analyze and question the source and the message. We worry as we prepare to move forward: "Was that really the
prompting of the Spirit or was it my own agenda? If it was the Spirit, I
need to act. If it was just me, then acting might lead to disaster."

The painful truth is that we may be able to quote scriptures or recite
a long list of Church history facts and stories; we might be serving
faithfully in our callings and regularly attending the temple; however,
when it comes time to listen for, recognize, and follow the quiet, subtle
whispers of the Spirit, we're often less confident. Of course, the working
of the Spirit is a very personal experience; only we know what we really
felt. Because it is so personal, it makes it impossible to get a second
opinion or to somehow rewind the prompting in order to listen to it

again. Those feelings, those swellings, become ours alone to clarify, understand, and follow.

I have sometimes thought it would have been easier had the Lord just "turned up the volume" on my promptings. Had I been in charge of designing this spiritual GPS system in the premortal life, I probably would have made sure promptings came with loud trumpets and flashing neon lights. Warnings would sound like blaring car alarms, wailing away until I paid attention to them.

And I would have been wrong. The Lord wanted us to quietly listen and feel and then to resolve and move forward. His voice would most often be communicated in stillness, in stirrings, and in joy and peacefulness. He didn't intend that it would generally be in the fire or the whirlwind. He intended for us to have to bend down, turn off the TV, and quietly seek to understand what is being whispered to us.

Several years ago I was asked to speak to a local Relief Society. When I asked for the topic they had in mind, they replied that they wanted me to speak on "Promptings or Me!" A number of the sisters in the ward worried about recognizing the Spirit in their decision making. When I spoke to them that night, we had a wonderful experience. The sisters came prepared and ready with questions and eager comments. The energy and spirit in the room was conducive to great discussions and a striving for answers.

At the end of the meeting, one young mother came forward with a look of relief on her face. "I just realized what I've been trying to do," she said with a sigh. "I was trying to use the Spirit to make sure I don't make mistakes!" She went on to explain that she was a perfectionist and had decided that if she could understand the Spirit better, she might be able to live a more perfect life. At the end of the class she realized the folly of trying to use those promptings as a spiritual backstop to her daily actions.

I believe that "prayer anxiety," not wanting to follow a false prompting, is partly a confirmation of our testimony in our Heavenly Father. We know that as Latter-day Saints we have been blessed with restored knowledge about God's character and attributes. We should be the most knowledgeable about the Spirit and its workings because of the increased revelations available to us. We know that it is the Light of Christ that was instrumental in helping us gain a testimony of the Book of Mormon. A full quarter of all our sacrament meetings are dedicated to the bearing of testimonies that came as a result of spiritual experiences. "Why then," we ask, "am I having such difficulty distinguishing between the Spirit and my own thoughts?"

One problem is that seasoned Saints can fail to recognize the Spirit too, even when it is speaking directly to them. We have two great examples from the Book of Mormon. In AD 34, "in the first month, on the fourth day of the month" (3 Nephi 8:5), at Passover, the new world was rocked with the massive upheaval and destruction following the death of the Savior in Jerusalem. Cities were destroyed, and the geography altered completely. The record states that the "more wicked" portion of the people were destroyed but that even the righteous suffered heavily due to the breadth of the storm's power and fury. Eventually the storm and destruction subsided, and the darkness finally parted. Survivors were left to ponder the destruction as well as the voice they'd heard. They then began the process of rebuilding.

Fully a year later, "in the ending of the thirty and fourth year" (3 Nephi 10:18), the people gathered again at the temple, again celebrating Passover. Truly, Passover, for these surviving Saints, would have taken on new meaning for those who had been "passed over" by the destruction a year earlier. Then, as they were comparing their experiences and were "marveling and wondering one with another" they "heard a voice as if it came out of heaven; and they cast their eyes round about, *for they understood not the voice which they heard*" (3 Nephi 11:1, 3).

We might pause here to remind ourselves of a couple of important points. First, these are the righteous survivors of the destruction a year previous. Their personal obedience had literally saved their lives. Second, they had continued to keep the commandments and were faithful in attending to the ordinances of the law of Moses. In addition, they had heard and recognized the voice from heaven a year ago. Now, these active, obedient "Nephite-day Saints" didn't recognize the voice speaking to them nor understand the message.

> And it was not a harsh voice, neither was it a loud voice; nevertheless, and notwithstanding it being *a small voice* it did pierce them that did hear to the center,
> And it came to pass that again they heard the voice, *and they understood it not.* (3 Nephi 11:3–4)

As these Nephite survivors could attest, *activity in the Church is no guarantee we will automatically understand the voice of the Spirit.* It can have a powerful effect on us, and still we miss it or assume we are feeling something else. Those at the temple felt the power; it pierced them to the core; it made them shake. But they still had to hear it repeated several times before they began to understand the message.

> And again the third time they did hear the voice, *and did open their ears to hear it; and their eyes were towards the sound thereof; and they did look.* . . .
>
> [*And*] *they did understand the voice.* (3 Nephi 11:5–6, emphasis added)

One problem for these traumatized Nephites was that they were not *facing* the voice. Though they were in the right place (the temple) at the right time (Passover), their focus appears to have been elsewhere.

Modern life and modern families stay extremely busy. Kids who play sports do not play just one sport, they play three or more sports and practice year round. Other organizations, in addition to family and church, clamor for time and attention. We manage to fill our lives with events and callings and families and work and a hundred other things. Thus, when the Spirit tries to whisper to us, we can easily be focused elsewhere. We might be the recipient of its effects but simply not take the time to face the voice and listen to its specific guidance. *For that reason, we may be feeling the Spirit but not understanding the voice.*

It is easy to focus on the wide sweep of the world as it flows around us on all sides. We are distracted by new or exciting events. Learning to screen out the distracting noise is not easy; it takes desire, combined with effort and practice. We may look in many directions except the one most helpful to us. It is for this reason that *we first need to recognize that we may be focused away from the very voice we wanted to hear.*

The Savior himself provided the second example of a people already receiving revelation and not being aware of it. When He visited the Nephites, He explained that the law of Moses was now fulfilled and animal sacrifices were no longer necessary. He then outlined the sacrificial requirements of the gospel of Jesus Christ.

> And ye shall offer for a sacrifice unto me a broken heart and a contrite spirit. And whoso cometh unto me with a broken heart and a contrite spirit, him will I baptize with fire and with the Holy Ghost, *even as the Lamanites,* because of their faith in me at the time of their conversion, were baptized with fire and with the Holy Ghost, *and they knew it not.* (3 Nephi 9:20)

The Anti-Nephi-Lehies were filled with the Holy Ghost at the time of their conversion, and they did not know it. *Their traditions had not prepared them to know what to look for.* They were never taught that the Holy Ghost would communicate to them, much less what it might feel like. Instead they had been taught only hate and anger toward their Nephite brethren. For King Lamoni and his people, understanding the Spirit—the Great Spirit—must have been a marvelous experience. No wonder they fainted on the spot!

In your circle of relationships—family, friends, ward members— you hear of spiritual experiences others have had. Many LDS homes are blessed with the legacy of parents or grandparents or pioneers who possessed great spiritual gifts. Their stories of "voices in the night" or dramatic, life-saving promptings may be part of sacred family lore.

The only difficulty with these important family experiences is that they can, unintentionally, create false expectations of what to expect for those who have not had this type of experience nor been given the same set of spiritual gifts. Our children need to be taught that while we cherish those great family prompting "traditions" (for they demonstrate the "great things the Lord has done for our fathers"), the spiritual gifts of family members will probably be different from our own individualized spiritual gifts. Not better, just different. Each of us has been blessed with our own spiritual talents.

Sometimes confusion is a result of waiting for the wrong manifestation of the Spirit. There has been a great deal of confusion in the Church regarding the "burning in the bosom" feeling (D&C 9:8). This experience is often suggested as the standard way for someone to know if the Book of Mormon is true. Unfortunately, many a Saint and investigator has waited in vain for the burning experience. When it does not happen, they might be led to conclude that either the book is *not* true or they are spiritually out of tune.

Speaking at a BYU devotional during Education Week, Elder Henry B. Eyring asked Saints to pay particular attention to their thought processes during his talk and subsequent classes. Said he:

> You can test what we have talked about today. What you do in the classes you attend . . . can build your foundation more solidly on truth. Just try two things: *listen for the whisperings of the Spirit and then commit to obey.* You've noticed . . . that from time to time your mind wandered away from what I was saying. God will take advan-

tage of that wandering if you let him.

... Write down impressions or thoughts that you feel came from God. ... Think carefully about whether the truth you received requires action. ... In this hour you may have committed to act on something you felt was true. ... *I fear that more people make promises to God than keep them*, so you will please Him when you are the exception and you keep your promise to obey.[3]

At times, we struggle with heavy issues. During the period of time we attend a Church meeting, the Holy Ghost may be present and powerful. At those moments we should take the initiative to draw our attention from the topic at hand and toward our particular problem. At those moments, if we will turn and "face" the voice, we may then be taught what it is the Lord needs for us to do. In addition, we may also understand more clearly what a prompting feels like.

Not long ago I invited a class to carefully follow President Eyring's challenge. I explained that during the course of my class we would talk about a number of sacred things. By virtue of our discussion, the Spirit would be there and bear witness of truth. But, I also explained that some might have come to class with specific questions or problems they needed answers for. During the course of my class, or other classes they might later attend, 1) the Spirit, 2) their righteous desires, and 3) their problem *would all be in the room at the same time*. In that setting, the Spirit might take the opportunity to provide them with the added light they were searching for. I challenged them to quickly write down their impressions, along with any commitments they agreed to make. In that way, they might find counsel and comfort regardless of the class topic.

Following that class, a sister came forward with some concerns she had recognized. During the class she found herself coming to some conclusions about how to proceed. As we visited, she described struggling with a decision for quite some time. She went on to say she now knew what she needed to do and had felt impressed to share it with me. Afterward she described the peace she felt. She had listened to the voice and was now fully committed to follow its directions.

A Challenge

In that vein, I would offer the same challenge to those who are reading this book. In all likelihood, you began reading because of personal issues you're anxious to find answers to. As you read, be aware that you may find your thoughts drifting toward a current situation or problem you're struggling with. Stop and feel for the gentle stirrings that might accompany this sudden detour. If your "sudden stroke of ideas"[4] is being accompanied by a sense of peace and calm, it could well be the Lord trying to provide you with answers. If this occurs, please stop and write down those impressions. Later, in prayer, seek confirmation from the Spirit on the directions you received.

A good example of these heavenly promptings comes from the life of Abraham Lincoln. In 1864, the Confederate army, under Robert E. Lee, moved into Pennsylvania. General Lee was determined to swing through Pennsylvania; turn south; capture Washington, DC; and perhaps end the war. When the Union army hurried to meet him at Gettysburg, it was understood by all sides exactly what the stakes were.

For that reason, President Lincoln's aides were surprised to find him unusually calm on the day prior to the deciding battle. After Gettysburg was won, President Lincoln was asked how he remained so peaceful at such a critical moment in history. He responded:

> In the pinch . . . when everybody seemed panic-stricken and nobody could tell what was going to happen, oppressed by the gravity of our affairs, I went to my room one day and locked the door and got down on my knees before Almighty God and prayed to Him mightily for victory at Gettysburg. I told Him that this war was His, and our cause His cause, but we couldn't stand another Fredericksburg or Chancellorsville. And I then and there I made a solemn vow to Almighty God that if He would stand by our boys at Gettysburg, I would stand by Him, and He did stand by [the] boys and I will stand by Him. And after that, I don't know how it was, and I cannot explain it, soon a sweet comfort crept into my soul. The feeling came that God had taken the whole business into His own hands and things would go right at Gettysburg, and that is why I had no fears about you.[5]

Knowledge and experience bring understanding. Learning to understand our promptings will take time and effort and sacrifice. Certainly, it is something we grow into over time. More importantly, we must desire to learn and to expand our spiritual sensitivity.

Occasionally another problem arises. Given the size of the decision, our fear is running rampant, and we don't want to ask Heavenly Father for something because the answer might be contrary to what we want.

Our reluctance to ask, in those cases, is not lack of experience but rather just the opposite. We have a sneaking suspicion that we know *exactly* what the Lord would have us do, and we feel uncomfortable or unprepared to do it. We hope He'll come up with something else!

At those moments, we may be looking in another direction *on purpose.* For the moment, we prefer our chosen course to the Lord's alternative. We believe we know our situation, we understand all the consequences, we have it worked out. Any answer other than ours will be inconvenient or difficult or embarrassing. It may require more work than we are willing to expend. *If I don't ask, then I'm not on the hook for the answer!* One wonders if the cry of "Nobody told me!" was heard rising up from the rubble of Sodom and Gomorrah as the fire began to rain down.

The fruits of the Spirit will bring joy; when we're filled with the Spirit, we are much happier than when we are not. Truman G. Madsen described an experience Hugh B. Brown had when he said, "He explained that we are to seek the Spirit as we seek the sun and bask in it against the day, inevitable, when we will be left to ourselves."[6]

In conclusion, we make our way across a lifetime of challenges and adventures. At times we feel completely lost and are not sure what to do next. If we are willing to withdraw from the bustle and demands of life and train ourselves to listen, we will be able to hear the voice of the Spirit trying to give us the help the Savior promised would be there for us. As we do so, we may discover an interesting truth: in all likelihood He has been speaking to us all along—we just needed ears to finally hear Him and the courage to follow.

Notes

1. Elden Watson, *Manuscript History of Brigham Young* (Salt Lake City: E. J. Watson, 1971), 529–31.
2. As told by Marion G. Romney, Conference Report, April 1944, 140–41.
3. Henry B. Eyring, "A Life Founded on Light and Truth," BYU Devotional, Aug. 15, 2000, 6.
4. Joseph Fielding Smith, *Teachings of the Prophet Joseph Smith* (Salt Lake City: Deseret Book, 1938), 151.
5. William Wolf, *The Almost Chosen People* (New York: Doubleday, 1958), 125.
6. Truman G. Madsen, "Hugh B. Brown—Youthful Veteran," *New Era*, April 1976, 15.

chapter seven

THE SPIRIT AND PERSONALITY TYPES

*I*t is human nature to compare ourselves with those around us. Without knowing the full range of another's circumstances, we quickly match what we know of ourselves with another's outward appearance or circumstance. The result can easily leave us prideful, fuel a sense of competition, or foster discontent. In general, little good ever comes from these inaccurate and unnecessary comparisons.

This is especially true in Church settings. We usually try to look and act our best in sacrament meeting, for instance. A client of mine described "putting on the sacrament meeting face" regardless of whatever else had been going on earlier in the day or week. Even with ward members we know well, we still don't know every challenge or struggle they battle and so we still might miss hidden strengths and challenges. We know only what we see and hear about and *think* we know. Our perception is our reality. Under those circumstances, it can be pretty difficult trying to keep up with the bishop's family or trying to *be* the bishop's family.

This tendency toward destructive comparisons can also affect what we're expecting when seeking for answers to prayers. I remember well a testimony meeting where a mother described a miraculous event from a recent family vacation. Potential disaster had been averted when she heard a voice tell her their camp trailer needed to be moved immediately. Despite the howls of inconvenience from her sleeping kids, the trailer was moved to a different spot. Later that night, a storm brought down a large tree limb that would have crushed their trailer had they left it where it was. This mother tearfully finished her experience by bearing her testimony of how grateful she was for the guidance of the Lord.

It was a wonderful testimony. She spoke of how her faith was strengthened and her children had received a powerful lesson of the importance of following the Spirit. As she finished speaking, though, I thought I saw some ward members looking away with a far-off look in their eyes and guessed what some were thinking. Rather than rejoicing with this sister, they thought: "Why is it that those kinds of experiences never happen to me? Is she more righteous than I am? Does the Lord love her more than He loves me? Where was that kind of help when our garage burned down?"

Unfortunately, this kind of thinking highlights perceived deficiencies in our own lives. It can be fueled by the tendency to think that *her* particular gift, the tangible yet quiet voice in her head, must be *the* way to receive the answers to prayer. We might be led to conclude that if we aren't receiving answers her way, there must be something wrong with us. We may then try to explain the seeming inequity by deciding we are unloved or unworthy! What we miss is the possibility that we have simply been given a different spiritual gift.

Growing up, I quickly learned that my mother was one of those "promptings" people. She tended to get impressions and feelings that she learned to follow. One evening, she and my father attended the temple. As they crossed the lobby toward the dressing room, she suddenly stopped. "Something's just not right with the family," she whispered to my father. "We need to go home." Immediately they turned around, walked back out to the car, drove the half hour back home, and then waited for the phone to ring. Within the hour, word came that my brother-in-law was being rushed to the hospital with painful kidney stones. His attack had begun about the time my parents arrived at the temple. To use a phrase from the movie *Star Wars*, my mother just knew something was wrong because there was "a disturbance in the Force!" While she heard no voice, there was a strong internal sense she had learned to recognize and was willing to follow.

Again, we hear these kinds of experiences and, if we're not careful, we can begin to assume that we are not "in tune" with the Spirit unless we have spiritual manifestations the same way others do. In truth, while my mother had those dramatic prompting moments, I generally do not. They are not my gift, and they may not be yours either.

After Joseph Smith began gathering the Saints to Kirtland, he discovered a peculiar problem among the Saints. Those living on the Western Reserve of Ohio, who had joined the Church as a group, had a lot of false expectations of how the Holy Ghost operates. These new Saints had come from a variety of Christian traditions and had a limited understanding of how to know that the Spirit was present. Because of those false traditions, they tended to be outwardly demonstrative with peculiar "gifts of the Spirit." It was not unusual for early Church meetings in Kirtland to be interrupted by loud and outlandish outbursts. Members might swoon or yell out or run around the room or pass out during meetings. Susan Easton Black describes Saints sitting on the floor, in the aisles, acting like they were rowing a canoe and shouting, "I'm on a mission to save the Lamanites!"[1] It took time and considerable effort for the Prophet to finally educate the Saints as to the true manifestations of the Spirit.

These traditions still exist in other faiths. My wife and I have a good friend who is a very devout member of another church. One Monday morning she came to work with a badly bruised arm and hand. When asked about it, she replied that her church "had been rocking" well into the night. She had beaten the walls of their little church when "the spirit" struck until she was left with bruises all up and down her arm. It is her understanding of how the Spirit works, and she's never known anything else.

Section 46 of the Doctrine and Covenants was given in Kirtland to help Saints better understand how the Spirit works and why. In it, the Lord outlined many kinds of spiritual gifts so that the Saints wouldn't be "seduced by evil spirits, or doctrines of devils, or the commandments of men" (D&C 46:7). It matched a similar list given by Paul in 1 Corinthians and by Moroni in Moroni 10. To counteract spiritual misunderstandings, we are all encouraged to "seek earnestly the best gifts, *always remembering for what they were given*" (D&C 46:8, emphasis added).

These gifts include the following:

> To some is given, by the Spirit of God, the word of wisdom.
>
> To another is given the word of knowledge, that all may be taught to be wise and to have knowledge.
>
> And again, to some it is given to have faith to be healed;
>
> And to others it is given to have faith to heal.
>
> And again, to some is given the working of miracles;
>
> And to others it is given to prophesy;
>
> And to others the discerning of spirits.
>
> And again, it is given to some to speak with tongues;
>
> And to another is given the interpretation of tongues. (D&C 46:17–25)

For what purpose are gifts of the Spirit given? The revelation actually answers that question. These gifts, these spiritual endowments, "are given for the benefit of those who love me and keep all my commandments; *and him that seeketh so to do* . . ." (v. 9). The gifts are meant to bless those who keep all the commandments—but especially those of us who are still trying! What a comforting phrase for those who are less than perfect but still trying.

In section 46, the Lord makes it clear that these heavenly strengths were meant to be scattered across the kingdom. "For all have not every gift given unto them," He declares, "for there are many gifts . . . to some is given one, and to some is given another, that all may be profited thereby" (vv. 11–12).

This spiritual dispersement provides each of us with varying sets of spiritual strengths and weaknesses. This causes us to have to work more closely with one other, relying on others' talents and blessings to offset our own weaknesses. The "pure in heart" need one another in order to be whole.

The diversity of spiritual gifts also helps explain why we have such great differences in how we receive answers to prayers. Over time you may have listened to the wide variety of ways other Saints describe how they feel the Spirit and receive their answers. As you do so, *realize again that there is no "right way" to receive promptings or answers to prayer.* Instead, there is *your* way, using *your* gift, as the Spirit works with *you.* Our goal should be, then, to become experts in how, specifically, the Lord uses our particular gifts to answer prayers and give us sacred knowledge.

Personality Types

Often, one way we may receive spiritual direction is through our own natural personality style. Each of us operates within four broad styles that help determine how we prioritize our lives. And while there are an endless number of combinations of these four, one style generally predominates. These personality styles explain a lot about how we work, socialize, and view the world around us. They also have major bearing on how we seek and respond to the Spirit. These four general categories are talkers, doers, thinkers, and planners. Let's briefly examine each area and its influence on our spiritual response.

Talkers. Talkers are social in nature and are driven to be with other talkers. Friendly and sociable, they love to surround themselves with friends. They draw energy from others. At Church they are outgoing and visible. Relationships with others are very important to them. One gift they may have is to "believe on [others] words," because they tend to be overly trusting.

A good example of one who drew heavy inspiration from friends and acquaintances was the Prophet Joseph Smith. Some might effectively argue that Joseph embodied all four personality areas. However, it was his "cheery personality" he used to best describe himself. Joseph drew heavily on the counsel and guidance of friends. I believe that his openness contributed greatly to the love others felt for him. Others loved him because they were first loved by him. They were also a constant source of inspiration for him in times of trial.

Talkers' spiritual strength lies in the fact that, because their emotional outlook is in relationships, they frequently have a natural tendency toward feeling the Spirit. It is in their emotional nature to be more aware of what they are feeling and to act on it. They are often the first, in any group, to be moved to tears by a spiritual experience.

Unfortunately, their spiritual weakness is also found in their friendships. Because they are so close to their friends, it is also natural for them to compare their spiritual experiences with others. As they compare, if they aren't careful, they may talk themselves out of the answers they've received. If their experience does not match their friends' experiences, they may doubt or second guess what it was they felt.

Doers. Doers are goal oriented, driven, bottom-line focused individuals. Impatient, they always want to be moving forward. They seek for the "bottom line" and become bored with endless details or descriptions. Their personal strengths lie in organizational manage-ment and administration. It is not unusual to see a doer functioning as the head of a company or organization. Their room or office is often filled with trophies, awards, and degrees placed prominently on their "ego wall." Even better is a picture taken of them with someone power-ful or famous.

For the doer, waiting for the Spirit to answer can be a frustrat-ing experience. We are often required to "wait on the Lord" as He provides guidance in His way and timetable. However, doers do not want to wait—ever! Preferring action, they might move too soon, but they are also more willing to take a prompting and run with it. The Lord explained, "if any man do my will, he will know of the doctrine." The leading quorums of the Church have been filled with doers who received answers "on the run," in the act of doing their duty.

Thinkers. Universities, CPA firms, law offices, labs, and computer companies are filled with thinkers. These individuals carefully exam-ine things, never moving quickly on a decision. They analyze and tear ideas apart. They critically examine points of view as well as their lawn mowers. They are always learning.

In the Church, thinkers are not easily satisfied with surface answers. Their constant questioning may even make some Church leaders uncomfortable. In spirituality, thinkers may have difficulty with spiri-tual answers because they are forced to rely on faith and feelings alone and not logical conclusions. That is uncomfortable ground for them. On the other hand, some thinkers, like Hugh Nibley, can be endlessly searching for additional knowledge and be pleased and strengthened by what they find.

One night, in a Relief Society enrichment night, I explained these four personality types to the sisters and then asked each group to go to a different corner of the room corresponding to their personality type. Four ladies immediately came up, frustrated and complaining they didn't know which of the four best described them. Laughing, I announced to the group, "if you wondered who your thinkers are, they're over here with me! They're still thinking and analyzing which corner they belong in!" They grinned, nodded, and then walked over to their corner. Later, after the meeting was over, I found them still exam-ining the characteristics of each group, still trying to be sure they really were thinkers. There was no doubt!

Planners. The world would cease to function without planners. They are our great organizers. They shun the limelight, preferring instead to set up, take down, take care of this, cook that, be responsible for that, and so forth. Quietly, without fanfare, they get things done. While talkers are talking and doers have already moved on, planners steadfastly make sure everything is getting done. After an activity, be assured, they will be the last ones to leave.

When it comes to spirituality, planners often understand spirituality through the service they provide. These are the times they feel the Spirit the most clearly. They simply need to find service projects because it is their native element. If there is a spiritual difficulty for planners, it is in their willingness to follow a prompting telling them to change a planned activity or to alter a prepared talk. Like thinkers, they are uncomfortable with spontaneity. In general, however, they love the security of the gospel and the organization of the Church. It is predictable and understandable. Truly, the kingdom of God on earth moves forward on the backs of quiet planners in every unit of the Church.

We tend to view decision-making through the prism of our personality type. For instance, a spiritual prompting that required immediate action would probably be immediately acted upon by a talker or doer; thinkers would have to spend some time analyzing the source and the message while the planner would first have to check with his or her schedule to make sure they could fit it in. The Lord knows how each of us will respond. He also knows our personality. For this reason, if a family were camped out under a tree, and the Lord wanted to warn the family that the tree was about to fall and the tent had to be moved, he would be less likely to prompt a thinker/father than he would a talker/ mother. In other words, heaven will communicate with us using our spiritual gifts and our natural personality.

Based on these factors, we might first look at places or situations where we received our last strong spiritual impression. Examples include

At the temple	Reading a book
On our knees	Talking to a friend
While driving	Reading the scriptures
While walking	In bed after the lights are out
Listening to a speaker	Listening to music

Personally, I am more likely to receive guidance while walking or driving and rarely while still on my knees. My wife finds counsel in opening up the scriptures, sometimes at random, and starting to read. Others I know will stay in the temple and find answers come best to them there. Each approach is different, involving spiritual gifts and unique personalities. The key is coming to know ourselves and then placing ourselves in places where we know we're more likely to be receptive to potential guidance.

When Not to Act

In addition to our personality type, we also need to be aware of when we are being "constrained" not to act. I worked once with a client seeking help with her depression. As we talked, she explained the sad set of circumstances that had begun her emotional slide downward. As a new convert she had had an inappropriate relationship with a missionary. Church disciplinary councils were held and both she and the missionary were excommunicated. To her credit, she remained close to the Church, moved out of state, and was actively preparing to be rebaptized. Her difficulty came as a result of additional incidents with the former missionary. He called her and then asked her to come visit with him. Once together, they immediately engaged in inappropriate behavior once again.

She knew that her baptism needed to be put off for now. She also blamed herself for giving in to old feelings and behaviors. In addition, she was confused about the former missionary. She confided to me that he was due to be rebaptized the following Friday night. When she had asked him about confessing to his bishop, he replied that it wasn't necessary since he was currently engaged to be married and would no longer be tempted.

Under the circumstances, I expected her to be angry and vengeful for his deceit. Instead, she was fearful of the eternal consequences should he be rebaptized unworthily. In order to help him and her, I agreed to intervene. As it turned out, the young man's former mission president actually lived in town. A call was made, and he agreed to meet with both her and myself.

During the interview, he asked some pointed and probing questions of my client. She supplied information to him about the original events that had never been disclosed at the time they occurred. He soon discovered that the former missionary had dishonestly down played the extent of their relationship from the very beginning. She was completely honest and straightforward about the latest indiscretions. It was a painful process, but I was very proud of her courage and candor.

After she was finished, the former mission president sat back and shook his head. "You know," he said with a long sigh, "I was aware he was being rebaptized this coming Friday. I've known it for a long time. In fact, I've had his rebaptism forms sitting on the corner of my desk for the past two weeks and I just never got around to sending them in. I'm usually a very organized person [a planner!], but for whatever reason I just couldn't do it. Now I know why. The Spirit was constraining me not to."

For this former mission president, to hold off on sending in the papers was far out of character for him. When he would try to send them in, he would "just not get around to it." Never, during those weeks, did he consider his lack of action was the Holy Ghost stopping him, but he did think his behavior odd and unusual. In this case, the spiritual prompting was felt more as a strong, compelling feeling—to do nothing! Only afterward was he able to identify it as spiritual intervention.

In conclusion, I believe that our lack of knowledge about the Holy Ghost and its spiritual manifestations is due to a number of factors. Many of us may be more in tune than we know, but we just don't "understand the voice" even when it is speaking to us. We may be turned in the wrong direction.

God has given us divine gifts of the Spirit. We haven't earned them, nor are we worthy of them when they are bestowed on us. They are given as gifts from a loving Father. They are designed to help us bless the lives of others we encounter in life. But these gifts also bless our lives because they can aid us in receiving answers to our prayers. They interact with our personality style to give us a unique pattern as to how we experience the Spirit. Since we are different from others we know, we cannot compare how we experience the voice of the Spirit with family and friends.

As we hone our spiritual gifts, we react to the voice of the Spirit with far more confidence and less hesitation. We are also more effective in recognizing when those "promptings" are a product of our own wants and wishes.

Note
1. Class notes in author's possession.

chapter eight

AFTER THE VISION CLOSES

> POOR SATAN—IT CAN'T BE MUCH FUN BEING A CHEERLEADER
> FOR A CHORUS OF CLONES, BUT HOW HE STAYS AT HIS TASK!
>
> NEAL A. MAXWELL

A number of prophets throughout history have been blessed with "The Vision." The Vision is a sweeping, panoramic vision of all God's creations. It is designed to teach, train, and inspire the Lord's oracles on earth. It has been experienced by prophets such as Abraham; Enoch; the brother of Jared; Peter, James, and John; Nephi; Mormon; and Joseph Smith.

One account of The Vision is found in the book of Moses. Moses was "caught up into an exceedingly high mountain" (Moses 1:1), where he was shown "the world and the ends thereof, and all the children of men which are, and which were created" (Moses 1:8). After the glory of this vision closed, Satan immediately pushed onto the scene and brazenly demanded, "Moses, son of man, worship me!" (Moses 1:12). For Moses, the difference in glory and power was dramatic and clear-cut. Satan's feeble demand paled next to the grandeur of the Lord and His endless creations. Moses was easily able to discern the difference and quickly refused.

However, Satan has never been one to back down easily—his pride does not let him. As he continued to demand obedience, loudly and insistently, from the astonished Moses, the record tells us, "And it came

77

to pass that *Moses began to fear* exceedingly; and as he began to fear, he saw the bitterness of hell" (Moses 1:20, emphasis added).

After four tries, Moses finally has to cast Satan out, but not before having an experience we should all remember when having our own mountaintop experiences. Moses's greatest struggle with the adversary came *after* his revelatory experience, not before. With images of The Vision still fresh in his brain, Moses had to face the power and might of evil despair and doubt.

Another person who understood well the experiences that come *after* revelatory moments was Oliver Cowdery. Sometime in April 1829, he was acting as scribe for the Prophet as they feverishly worked to complete the translation of the Book of Mormon. At some point, Oliver sought for a chance to translate as well. The Lord apparently gave him permission to do so, explaining, "I will tell you in your mind and in your heart [how to translate] by the Holy Ghost, which shall come upon you and which shall dwell in your heart . . . therefore this is thy gift" (D&C 8:2, 4).

With that endorsement, Oliver attempted to translate but failed after a brief period. The Lord then takes back the gift, giving two reasons why Oliver was not successful. First, "You have supposed that I would give it unto you, when you took no thought save it was to ask me" (D&C 9:7). In other words, Oliver assumed that it would simply flow as easily as it appeared to flow from the mouth of Joseph Smith. The second problem was even more basic than that. He was told the gift had been taken from him because "you did not continue as you commenced, when you began to translate. . . . Behold it was expedient when you commenced; *but you feared*, and the time is past" (vv. 5, 11, emphasis added).

As with Moses, revelation to proceed forward with something the Lord has directed was soon followed by feelings of fear and doubt. Rather than continue, Oliver allowed that fear to stop his efforts. Surely, he could have learned a lesson from Joseph, who knew what it meant to face fear and terror both before *and after* the First Vision.

We might ask what it is about fear and doubt that drives the Spirit of revelation away after we've felt it. Alma explains that we are to be "led by the Holy Spirit, becoming meek, submissive, patient, full of love" (Alma 13: 28). In addition, "perfect love casteth out all fear" (Moroni 8:16). Heavenly communication results in our being filled with love.

His guidance is truly a gift from above. It is proof that by the Holy Ghost we can "know the truth of all things" (Moroni 10:5).

Conversely, "perfect fear casteth out love." The two elements, love and fear, are polar opposites. By its very nature, fear drives enlightenment and peace away. As we fill with fear and despair, we focus on the negative things that can happen or might happen and exclude the wonderful things the Lord can do for us.

Brigham Young wanted to begin to build the Salt Lake Temple from the moment the pioneers entered the valley. He soon found he had very little support for that idea, however. When he inquired, he found that it wasn't the actual work of construction his brethren objected to. What they feared more was the evil opposition that they'd always experienced while building temples. These seasoned leaders were well aware that each time they had begun to build, persecution quickly mounted and soon they were being evicted from their homes. They'd seen it in Kirtland, Missouri, and Nauvoo. They didn't relish the idea of having to leave the Salt Lake Valley so soon after getting there! Responding to their fears, Brigham said:

"Some say, 'I do not like to do it, for we never began to build a Temple without the bells of hell beginning to ring.' I want to hear them ring again. All the tribes of hell will be on the move, if we uncover the walls of this Temple. But what do you think it will amount to? You have all the time seen what it has amounted to."[1]

Any time the kingdom of God moves forward, as a Church or individually, we should not be surprised when opposition arrives. In fact, the negative response we may receive could be part of the gospel plan the Lord intends for our growth. As Lehi explained, "For it must needs be, that there is an opposition in all things. If not so, my firstborn in the wilderness, righteousness could not be brought to pass, neither wickedness, neither holiness nor misery, neither good nor bad" (2 Nephi 2:11).

Opposition does and will manifest itself after we commit to an inspired course of action. The Apostle Peter experienced a powerful object lesson on keeping his focus on the Savior despite the opposition around him. On a stormy night, the disciples had sailed across the Sea of Galilee while the Savior stayed behind to pray. A fierce storm began and threatened to sink the small boat. At the moment when destruction looked inevitable, they spotted a figure walking across the water toward them. As they struggled to recognize their Master, He called out: "It is I; be not afraid" (Matthew 14:27).

If we are not careful, we might have a tendency to pass quickly over this familiar story, summarizing it with a simple, "Peter tried to walk on the water and failed." In wonderful actuality, Peter succeeded. Through his faith in Christ, this humble fisherman performed a great miracle, defied physics, and walked across the Sea of Galilee. As long as he focused on his Savior, he defied the deep and moved through the storm toward Him. The elements had no effect. It was only when Peter began to fear that the Spirit that had buoyed him retreated, and he then did what mortals do on their own: he fell. The "bitterness of hell" drew him away from the peace and safety he'd known a minute before, and he plunged into the thing he was most worried about.

What is less noticed about Peter's experience is the wind. The boat struggled to get across the sea because the wind and weather were "contrary," meaning it was blowing in the opposite direction the disciples were desiring to go. Then, as Peter begins to step across the waves, the scripture records that the wind driving the waves had become "boisterous"—meaning, I take it, that it had become worse. It is probably this change that catches Peter by surprise, causing the fear and doubts that sink him.

Finally, after he and the Savior have successfully returned back to the boat, the account simply concludes that the wind "ceased." Ceased! I can picture Peter taking a moment to turn to the Savior and say, in effect, "Dear Master, I know you are the Master of earth and seas. Had you chosen to do so, you could have calmed the sea and caused the wind to cease before I started walking. I may have never feared or started to fall. Instead, you allowed it to get worse. I'm just wondering . . . why did you do that?"

And just as surely we can imagine the Lord's probable reply, "Peter, I love you and know what you need to learn. Soon you'll bear the heavy load of leadership. I need you to know that I will be there even if the sea you walk on grows more threatening—as it surely will. You now know that when that happens I will be there and will lift you up immediately. Don't let fear cause you to lose your focus."

The Savior could have made Peter's walk easier had He chosen to, but he needed Peter to learn another important lesson: that none of us have the assurance that our path will become easier immediately after following divine guidance. Rather, sacred history is replete with constant examples of men and women who did receive answers to prayers but had to endure a season of difficulty afterward.

This concept of increased adversity after receiving answers to prayers can be a difficult pill to swallow. In our trials, we turn to the Lord, hoping that we will receive relief and peace. That is one of the prime reasons we pray. To have tribulations get even worse in response may certainly seem unfair.

Perhaps we can find a measure of comfort in the same verse that sent a fourteen-year-old boy into the woods to pray. "If any of you lack wisdom," James invites, "let him ask of God, that giveth to all men liberally, and upbraideth not; and it shall be given him" (James 1:5). But if we are not careful, we might also miss the condition attached to that promise. He explains there are conditions that can render a prayer unanswered. "But let him [who asks] ask in faith, *nothing wavering*. For he that wavereth is like a wave of the sea driven with the wind and tossed." And then this final warning from James: "For let not that man [who wavered] think that he shall receive any thing of the Lord" (James 1:6–7, emphasis added).

Being "tossed to and fro" can occur before we receive an answer to prayer, but I believe we are especially vulnerable to doubt when results appear to be worse afterward. If we then waver, we can be impacted by any wave of opinion that comes our way. Lacking an anchoring determination, we may begin to drift off course, completely at the mercy of the sea and "contrary" winds. James also describes this lack of direction as "double minded" (James 1:8).

Imagine the same situation had Peter wavered. Like us, he might have called out to the Lord, double checking to be sure it was really Him. Then, upon hearing the answer "Come!" he may have lingered in the boat a little longer, stalling as he built up his courage. *Maybe I need to be sure it really is the Lord*, he thinks. *The waves are pretty high, and I could get hurt here if I'm not careful.* He calls out again, and again the invitation is extended. Finally, with a nervous look around, he gingerly steps over the side and places a trembling foot on the water. It holds! Still clinging to the side of the boat, he slides out a little ways, checking all the while that he's not falling through. Suddenly a wave splashes over his foot and soaks his ankle. The bottom of his robe gets wet. With a bound, he jumps back into the boat and decides it would be safer to wait for the Savior to arrive. "I probably could have done it," he tells his companions, "but it is tough out there! And how would any of you know? You didn't try it!"

Unfortunately, many of us waver with the Spirit's warmth still lingering in our hearts. The storm comes, with all its fury, pressing down and disturbing what we've just been told. Intellectual arguments fill our mind, explaining, logically, why the inspired course of action would not be wise. We see the coming difficulties and doubt our abilities. We second guess the source. And the longer we examine all these ramifications, the more anxiety and fear creep in. Pretty soon we begin to sink below the waves.

I always jokingly explained to my clients that there is a part of our brain neurosurgeons can never find with a CT scan: it is called our awfulizer. Its job is to evaluate all the possibilities in any new situation and immediately paint a picture of the worse outcome possible. The result will be just awful! For instance, a boy bouncing a ball in the house can do a lot of damage. But it is his mother, reacting with the overdeveloped awfulizer (mother version) who calls out, "Don't bounce that ball in the house, you'll put someone's eye out!"

When we focus on fear, we begin to sense the bitterness of hell that Moses saw (Moses 1:20). It dominates and drives love and peace away. The feelings associated with our heavenly answer fade into a distant memory. The water is lapping at our feet, and the storm is raging. If we did not anticipate the inevitable doubt or think that our situation might worsen, the fear takes us by surprise. Thus we still huddle in the boat, knowing there might be direction to follow but deciding to wait for the storm to stop. And as we do so, we drift farther and farther away from our intended shore.

The Log Cross

As a ropes course facilitator, I frequently used an experiential activity called the "log cross" to teach a powerful lesson. It is as simple as it is impactful. My clients would walk across a horizontal log, fifty feet long, while maintaining their balance. The log could be on the ground or it could be hanging thirty feet in the air; the result is the same.

I would have an individual stand on one end of the log, looking across to the other end. I would have him close his eyes, visualizing

something he wanted most in his life. I would have him describe that wish in great detail, vividly picturing it in his mind. He might envision a happier marriage or a depression-free life. He would then open his eyes and picture his desired object at the far end of the log. The only thing that would separate him from the things he wanted was a determined, focused walk to the other side. What became immediately apparent was that the things we want most usually require us to leave the safety and comfort of our present situation and risk moving forward.

Most participants began by gathering themselves, focusing, and then slowly, carefully beginning to walk. Step by step they moved toward the picture they'd visualized. As they walked, though, I would intervene. I stood behind them, calling out all the negative and destructive things they told me they believed about themselves. I simply reminded them, using their own words, of the fears and self doubts that replayed, constantly, in their heads. *I'm not really smart. Everyone thinks I'm stupid. No one will ever love me.* The farther they walked, the louder I became. With each step, I would question—as they did—their ability to actually accomplish their goal. It never took very long to activate their mental awfulizer!

Predictably, about halfway across the log, they would pause. Then their balance would falter a little. Next, they would shift their focus away from their goal and nervously begin glancing at others in the group or back at me. At that point, I knew it was just a matter of time before they'd fall.

On the other hand, I've had other participants who started across the same expanse of log. These, however, refused to be distracted. They maintained their focus and walked quickly toward what it was they cherished. They refused to lose focus regardless of the negative chatter around them.

As we move forward with a prompting, we duplicate Peter's walk on the water. His walk is our walk. The message is deceptively and amazingly simple: look to the Savior and live; focus on our fears and fall—regardless of the storm swirling around us.

Prior to his experience with translating, Oliver Cowdery was taught another lesson about how the Spirit works. He first learned about the Book of Mormon while teaching school in Palmyra. After hearing stories about Joseph Smith and the plates of gold, he visited with the Smith family. They confided that Joseph and Emma were living in Harmony and attempting to translate the record, but the work was moving slowly due to the lack of a consistent scribe. Emma had tried, as had others, but it was not working. Shortly afterward, the Spirit whispered to Oliver that he would be the scribe Joseph needed to complete the work.

Filled with determination, Oliver soon made the journey to meet Joseph and Emma. When he arrived, Oliver desired a revelation, through Joseph, confirming the fact that he was to assist in the translation. The revelation was received, and Oliver was called to work with Joseph on the book. But, before he began, the Lord wanted to teach Oliver about how personal revelation works.

Said the Lord:

> Thou hast inquired of me, and behold, as often as thou hast inquired *thou hast received instruction of my Spirit.* If it had not been so, thou wouldst not have come to the place where thou art at this time.
>
> Behold, thou knowest that thou hast inquired of me and *I did enlighten thy mind;* and now I tell thee these things that thou mayest know that thou hast been enlightened by the Spirit of truth;
>
> Yea, I tell thee, that thou mayest know that there is none else save God that knowest thy thoughts and the intents of thy heart.
>
> Verily, verily, I say unto you, if you desire a further witness, *cast your mind upon the night that you cried unto me in your heart,* that you might know concerning the truth of these things.
>
> *Did I not speak peace to your mind concerning the matter?* What

greater witness can you have than from God? (D&C 6:14–16, 22–23, emphasis added)

Put another way, the Lord might have said, "The answer you received that night in Palmyra *was* revelation to you, just as much as the revelation received through my servant Joseph. If you have felt the Spirit you have heard me!"

Oliver's problem is a common one. We go to the Lord for help. In response, the still, small voice whispers guidance and counsel. But then we hesitate. One reason we might hesitate is that, in the past, we may have met disaster after obeying such a prompting. When that happened, we sifted through the wreckage and began second guessing. In our minds, the negative result was proof we were out of tune and in need of repair, whether we were or not. For people who are attempting to live by the Spirit, these outcomes seriously hamper their confidence in following spiritual promptings.

However, as we've discussed, prophets throughout the ages have testified that discouraging moments occur as we spiritually mature. As we learn the walk of faith, we risk being wrong from time to time. But it is a walk we must take if we want to learn to distinguish and follow the still, small voice. The measure of our faith is not in never being wrong, it is in following the Spirit through sunshine and rain and boisterous waves. Through the process, we learn that "obedience" to the Spirit "is better than [the] sacrifice" of our perfection (see 1 Samuel 15:22).

A few years ago, a good friend called me up one night. "I think I want to become a Mormon," he said. As we talked, it was clear that he had been touched by visits to my family and the spirit he felt in our home. I arranged for him to meet the missionaries and begin the lessons. As he was taught, he read a great deal. He especially enjoyed his visits to "The Honeybee Store" (Deseret Book). He looked happier than I had ever known him. The glow was noticeable to everyone who knew him, even nonmembers.

Finally, he was baptized in front of a large group of Saints and soon received the Aaronic Priesthood. Unfortunately, a few months later, he began to be conflicted by extended family and other "voices" who slowly began to chip away at his newfound confidence. Ultimately, despite all our efforts, his "glow" faded and he left the Church altogether.

Friendly Fire

Guidance from the Holy Ghost can also come under attack by well-intentioned friends and family. There is never a shortage of free advice from those who care about you. They instinctively seek to reduce your pain. And yet, while they have been observing your trials, they have not been there as you "toiled upward in the night."[2] They cannot know what you've felt and learned. From a "window shopping" perspective, they did not hear the Savior's invitation to you to "come!" Without this knowledge, they cry out loudly as you step over the side of the boat during the storm.

Family and friends are a powerful support as we move forward with our decisions. We need their help and their love. Conversely, they can also be part of the waves that toss us about as we waver. In their efforts to help, they propose alternatives to the inspired guidance we've received. Not wanting to hurt their feelings, we respond by giving their suggestions serious consideration. In the process of receiving this "friendly fire," we may end up grieving the Spirit rather than insulting family and friends.

There is a place for helpful counsel prior to—and after—receiving spiritual answers. When I was a member of a bishopric, we always discussed whom the Lord might want to serve in a particular calling. Sometimes we would disagree about choices or skills or the type of person needed. At the end of the discussion, we would kneel in prayer with our best decision. If we still felt unsettled, and sometimes we did, the discussion would continue. If we received a calm assurance that the Lord had made His choice, the discussion stopped and we moved forward. There were times, watching someone struggle in a calling, that I had to remind myself of the answer we'd received.

Our personal decision-making process can be just like a bishopric making a decision. We do not discount the experience and knowledge of those who may have helpful insights into our areas of decision. But there is a point when the answer has been received and action follows. Our actions may or may not conform to the steps recommended by those who provided advice. We must simply choose the Lord, who knows all things, over those who don't.

In conclusion, the process of following our promptings can be more difficult than receiving them. The Lord has great things in store, but they will require us to move beyond our places of comfort. Inspired guidance may involve taking bold but inspired actions as we walk across waves that may turn contrary, testing our resolve. However, if we will keep our eyes fixed on the Savior and keep moving, we will find everything He has in store for us.

Note

1. Brigham Young, *Deseret News*, Apr. 10, 1861, 41.
2. Henry Wadsworth Longfellow, quoted in Brad Wilcox, *The Continuous Atonement* (Salt Lake City, Deseret Book, 2009).

chapter nine

LESS-THAN-DIVINE ANSWERS

*I*n chapter eight, we talked of the importance of following divine answers we receive in prayer in spite of the doubt and opposition that may rush in afterward. Unfortunately, *there are times when it was not right in the first place.* I'm aware of two returned missionaries who were dating the same girl. Within a week, both men revealed to the girl that they had prayed about marriage and *both* explained that she was the one! Her response was that she'd prayed and *neither* was the one! So, three prayers, three different answers. Who was right?

These matrimonial mis-revelations are but an example of a far larger problem. Two worthy, well-intentioned young men believed they had been given inspiration. Both had felt *something*. However, both, apparently, were wrong and being influenced by factors other than the Spirit. The fact that we sometimes receive an answer we're not sure of can cause more concern than answers never received. Promptings from the Lord should be a call to action, to break camp and boldly head down the trail. Once we are traveling, we sometimes begin to question whether the "revelation" was inspired or not. In the last chapter we talked about the importance of moving forward. However, if we really do determine it was not of the Holy Ghost, we also might begin to doubt our spiritual ability. Were we deceived?

False promptings can come from a variety of sources. A friend of mine recently married into a family where his new father-in-law was renowned for his spiritual gifts. The family bragged on the many times he'd responded, on a moment's notice, to divine instructions to do things. It became a source of family pride. One afternoon he suddenly announced that an earthquake would soon level a portion of their small rural town and that their house was in the path of destruction. Over the next weekend, he demanded his family move all their belongings to a newly rented house in another town, far away from the upcoming danger zone.

The ward's elders quorum turned out to help, understanding simply that the family was moving. When the foretold date of the earthquake came and went, the family quietly moved their belongings back to the house. The father visited his doctor not long afterward and was finally diagnosed with bipolar disorder, a mental condition that can bring on hallucinations and psychotic thinking. In the process, the shaken family began to dramatically reassess his entire history of revelations and visions.

In a much darker sense, there are also those whose "promptings" affect not only themselves but also others who share in them. These people claim "revelations" for others or for the Church, prophesying of events to come. At the bottom of any apostate claim is generally an "impression," "vision," "dream," or "revelation" to justify their actions. The scriptures and Church history are replete with charismatic Korihors who find the Church at fault while they, alone, have the revelatory answer. Some of these visionaries make up revelations to suit their purposes, but others legitimately, honestly believe they've received heavenly counsel and zealously act on it.

In essence, promptings can come from a wide variety of sources that are not so divine. They can disrupt our sincere efforts to get actual answers and leave us tentative when we receive future ones. Some are very clearly Satan's efforts to sever our relationship with God, but many are not. They come, and we misinterpret due to lack of experience or spiritual acuity. Regardless, most can leave us spiritually shaken when we discover we acted on false guidance.

The Lord gives us guidelines on the alternate voices that can confuse us. Earlier, we talked of the spiritual mayhem the Church experienced in the early days of Kirtland. Many manifestations were bizarre, disruptive, and based on the traditions and understandings of the new converts. Joseph Smith inquired of the Lord on how to educate without offending. In response, he was given direction that helps differentiate the sources that may prompt us:

> But, ye are commanded in all things to ask God, who giveth liberally; and that which the Spirit testifies unto you even so I would that ye should do in all holiness of heart, walking uprightly before me, considering the end of your salvation, doing all things with prayer and thanksgiving . . . that ye may not be seduced by [1] *evil spirits,* [2] *doctrines of devils, or* [3] *the commandments of men.* . . .
>
> Wherefore beware lest ye are deceived; and that ye may not be deceived seek ye earnestly the best gifts. . . ." (D&C 46:7–8, emphasis added)

False revelations can come from any of these three sources. Let's look at them one at a time, "lest ye are deceived."

Evil Spirits

One of the more common Mormon myths, innocently perpetuated in the Church, is the two-plan theory of the premortal life. The primary version sounds like this:

"In the Council in Heaven, Jesus had a plan and Satan had a plan. The people voted for Jesus's plan. Satan and his followers were mad, and there was a war in heaven. Satan lost, and he and his people were cast out of heaven."

The problem with this simplistic explanation is how inaccurate it is. The more accurate primary version would sound something like this:

Before we came to this earth, we lived with Heavenly Father. We wanted to become like Him. He taught us about the eternal plan of happiness that would enable us to become like He is. It meant that we would come to earth and make mistakes while we learn and prove we could keep the commandments. Heavenly Father's plan included our eldest brother, Jesus Christ, who would come to this earth and make it so that those sins could be erased if we did everything we could do. Jesus said He would do everything Father in Heaven asked Him to. Another elder brother, Lucifer, also wanted to be like God. Only he didn't want to go through the work and pain of earth life. He also didn't want to die on the cross. He wanted God's glory immediately. He flattered a lot of others into following him. Pretty soon he began saying mean things about Jesus and those who followed Him. Lucifer and his followers rebelled and attempted to take our agency. As a result, they were cast out of heaven and lost their opportunity to gain a body.

In truth, there was one eternal plan presented and sustained, similar to the weekly sustaining we do in sacrament meeting. There was no viable second plan, only a rebellion against the plan of happiness and the One chosen as Savior.

And that rebellion continues today. Those who rebelled rebel still. They are still at war with those who fought against them and are determined to rob us of our agency. In the dark math of Satanomics, the disruption of one righteous life cascades down the countless generations. Confusion confuses exponentially!

As we look at possible sources of false promptings, evil spirits are distinguishable due to the dark feelings of anger and malice that are so apparent when they are around. But we shouldn't be surprised by evil interventions that intrude before a significant calling or answer to prayer. Their influence leaves one feeling their despair and darkness. It is a stark contrast to the peace and calm that attends the Comforter. Like Moses, we compare and ask, "where is thy glory?" (Moses 1:13).

On the other hand, Satan also has "gifts of the spirit" that are subtle and more difficult to distinguish. These seductive outpourings are what the Lord identifies as doctrines of devils.

Doctrines of Devils

"That ye may not be deceived," the Lord told Joseph Smith, "seek ye earnestly the best gifts, always remembering for what they are given . . ." for "they are given for the benefit of those who love me and keep my commandments" (D&C 46:8, 9). While the Lord's gifts benefit His children who love Him, Satan's spiritual arsenal is designed to benefit Satan, as it always does. His doctrines carefully lead man to "choose eternal death, according to the evil which is therein . . . to captivate, to bring you down to hell" (2 Nephi 2:29). What are these doctrines of devils and how do they invade our promptings? Paul helps us understand them:

Now the Spirit speaketh expressly, that in the latter times some shall depart from the faith, *giving heed to seducing spirits, and doctrines of devils*;

Speaking lies in hypocrisy; having their conscience seared with a hot iron;

Forbidding to marry, and commanding to abstain from meats, which God hath created to be received with thanksgiving of them which believe and know the truth. (1 Timothy 4:1–3, emphasis added)

Doctrines of devils come from the "father of lies" but sound pleasing to the natural man. Wrapped in godly looking paper, they are tied up with a bow of truth. Elder Bruce R. McConkie warned that these lies would be taught by false teachers "speaking lies in hypocrisy." Said he, "Knowing full well that their words are false, they will yet send them forth because they are pleasing to the carnal mind."[1]

Doctrines such as "forbidding to marry and commanding to abstain from meats" are examples of causes that might sound noble and god-given to some, filling its adherents with a smug sense of superiority over the unenlightened. Intellectually charged, these doctrines can cause true believers to "read by the lamp of their own conceit,"[2] even while living prophets are declaring otherwise.

Sadly, those who have bought into these dangerous doctrines often begin to believe their false illumination. "I taught them," they say, "even until I had much success, insomuch that I verily believed that they were true" (Alma 30:53). Lies that can be told using the name of God are powerful deceivers—even of the "very elect" (Matthew 24:24).

Notice that they will be successful "for a season." While this season may be short, a great deal of damage can be done during that season. There is great pain and loss for those who follow these lies, who sell their birthright for intellectual potage, only to discover the falsehood when great damage has been done. By this time, decisions have been made and lives altered. Only when the light shines completely on these follies is the full extent of the deception realized.

I was taught, early in Primary, that not "taking the Lord's name in vain" (Exodus 20:7) meant not swearing, especially using the Lord's name while doing so. However, taking the Lord's name vainly has a much more destructive meaning. Each time false prophets commit evil acts, deceiving their followers and declaring God's approval, they have taken His name vainly. For instance, the history of slavery in the

United States cannot be told without mentioning the horrible atrocities committed by the Ku Klux Klan. Wearing crosses on their robes, they claimed to be doing God's will. Surely, a harsh judgment awaits those who hid behind the Savior's name as they terrorized children of God.

How do we know when an inspiration or prompting is actually a doctrine of the devil? One sure way to know is when it leads us to paths contrary to what the prophet and the Church currently teach. Personal revelations that direct us to "higher" or "special" callings, to things the rest of the Church is not "prepared for" are doctrines of the devil. They are seductive in their appeal to pride. In addition, they harden hearts and make it difficult for the deceived to return.

As a deacon, I was blessed with a devoted youth leader. He magnified his calling and helped make our activities fun and meaningful. Friendly and outgoing, he was involved in many leadership positions. Then, tragedy struck. With little warning, his wife of ten years suddenly left him and their three daughters. When he finally found her, she had joined a fringe group still clinging to plural marriage. She explained to him that she had received a "revelation" that she was now ready to live a "higher law" while the rest of the Church was just not prepared to do so. She explained that this would involve certain "sacrifices," such as abandoning her family, but she was now prepared to follow. Satan had appealed to her pride, causing her to make some catastrophic choices.

Elder Oaks warns against those "other voices [that] are the bleats of lost souls who cannot hear the voice of the Shepherd and trot about trying to find their way without his guidance. Some of these voices call out guidance for others—*the lost leading the lost.*"[3]

Commandments of Men

The final source of alternate promptings is the commandments of men. These persuasions can confuse our perception of the still, small voice. In its place we may be feeling the influences of others or the pandering of our own personal desires.

Commandments or influences of others. In 1832, the Prophet Joseph dictated the first of four versions of the First Vision. In it he describes his state of mind prior to that historic prayer:

> At about the age of twelve years my mind became seriously imprest with regard to the all important concerns for the wellfare of

my immortal Soul which led me to Searching the Scriptures believeing as I was taught, that they contained the word of God thus applying myself to them and my intimate acquaintance with those of differant denominations led me to marvel excedingly for I discovered that they did not adorn their profession by a holy walk and Godly conversation agreeable to what I found contained in that Sacred depository this was a grief to my Soul thus from the age of twelve years to fifteen I pondered many things in my heart concerning the sittuation of the world of mankind the contentions and divions the wickeness and abominations and the darkness which pervaded the minds of mankind *my mind become excedingly distressed for I became convicted of my Sins.*[4]

He simply wanted to know where and how to have his sins remitted. The great restoration began with a question and a prayer. In response, he was told that the answers he sought were not to be found among the teachers of the day. The Lord warned him that "they draw near to me with their lips, but their hearts are far from me, *they teach for doctrines the commandments of men*, having a form of godliness, but they deny the power thereof" (JS-H 1:19).

The commandments of men appear to be of God; in reality, their power and logic is strictly mortal—as are their hearts and motivations! They sound authoritative and highly persuasive as they weave a compelling story. Several years ago my wife and I were invited to join a new multi-level marketing company. We were shown around the palatial home of the company's top salesman. In response to a question about the Church and his business, the salesman proudly proclaimed, "The Church loves this company; in fact, the Lord loves this company! Think how much tithing we pay!" Needless to say we chose not to involve ourselves with the company or this individual.

Well-polished, emotional appeals can stir us in the moment and lead to decisions we wouldn't make otherwise. In the process of making that decision, their logic still ringing in our ears, we may feel excited or motivated and mistake those feelings for the Spirit. Later on, when the damage is done, we better understand the Lord when He reminds us that we "have gone on in the persuasions of men. For behold you should not have feared man more than God" (D&C 3:6, 7).

Similar "commandments" can come in the form of pressure to get an answer that pleases someone else. For instance, the father of a young family is offered a job that would require a move out of state. This would move his wife close to her family and the children closer to their cousins. The husband, though, has never really enjoyed his in-laws and secretly appreciated the distance from them. In this case, both husband and wife have a vested interest in the outcome of the prayer. In the process of praying, this couple gets a mixed answer: the husband that they should turn down the offer while the wife feels strongly they should move.

The ensuing discussion is filled with arguments for and against the move. Personal feelings and opinions sway their feelings and color their interpretation of each other's promptings. Completely left out of their discussion is a humble willingness to go wherever the Lord directs, even if it means their spouse "wins." Too many prayers are decided by the dominant spouse, who then trumps a claim of spiritual endorsement.

Commandments of self-persuasion. Finally, false inspiration can also come from listening to what our natural man or woman thinks he or she wants. These self-fulfilling revelations are always pleasing because they tell us exactly what we wanted to hear. Of all the sources of false inspiration, this may be the most difficult to discern.

In attempting to distinguish between the Lord's answers and our own desires, we should carefully consider these six questions, proposed by Elder Hartman Rector,[5] that help determine the source of our inspiration. We should ask,

1. *"Is it within the bounds and limitations of your calling, and does it require a service consistent with your calling?"* In other words, is the answer intended only for us or for those we have responsibility over? When we receive answers for someone else's stewardship, we can be assured those answers are not from God. He does not work that way.

2. *"Is it consistent with the revealed word of God?"* As we discussed above, doctrines of the devil look like inspiration but subtly lead in paths opposite from the revealed word of God. Answers that gratify our pride or exalt us in the eyes of others are the kind of answers Satan knows will appeal to the vain. Hidden or secret knowledge, unavailable to the rest of the Church, is not among the consistent established patterns of the kingdom of God on earth.

3. *"[Are you] a fit receptacle?"* This question not only is about repentance, it also concerns the desires of our heart. When we sought our

answer, how meek were we? Were we willing to submit to whatever the Lord would direct, or did we approach Him with a limited list of things we'd do? Did we set a strict timetable based on the situation as we know it, or did we defer to a Heavenly Father for whom "all things are present before mine eyes"? (D&C 38:2).

4. *"Does the communication edify and cause you to rejoice?"* Whenever we are in contact with the Spirit, we always experience an increase of love. The love of Christ fills us and will aid us in what we've been directed to do. Answers that leave us depressed or sad or angry should be seriously questioned. Gratitude is a natural response to divine direction. "Rejoice, O my heart," declares Nephi, "and give place no more for the enemy of my soul" (2 Nephi 4:28).

5. *"Does it . . . speak peace to your soul, or are you left troubled by the communication?"* The Holy Ghost is the comforter the Savior promised to the world. This comforter will provide peace to our hearts as answers are received. Answers from other sources cannot duplicate heavenly peace; this feeling of love is unique to divine confirmation.

6. *"Is the communication vivid to the understanding, or does it leave a cloud or a hazy impression?"* Spiritual answers give us a calm, clear path to follow. They expand our mind as we understand what we are to do. This is generally accompanied by a sense of relief as our conflict is resolved. This is true even if the answer is contrary to what we expected—the calm is the same.

Many parents struggle and mourn over children who wander from their Church moorings. Mothers and fathers can plead "with all the feeling of a tender parent, that they would hearken" (1 Nephi 8:37), but to no avail. Sleepless nights are spent trying to formulate a response to rebellious answers and behaviors. Decisions about how to apply consequences can be difficult to formulate. At those moments every action seems doomed to failure. Wayward kids seem to do better finding self-destruction than their parents and Church leaders do at stopping them.

An additional problem may arise when a desperate parent approaches the Lord still smarting from angry or hurt feelings. These feelings can easily stand in the way of clearly understanding a heavenly response. Bruised egos seek justice, not mercy. A forgiving Father does not endorse punitive actions based on revenge. Parents who rise from their knees with a calm, clear vision do not have hearts filled with resentment or anger.

Separating out our own emotional reactions from the calming presence of the Holy Ghost requires experience and the gift of discernment. There is a dramatic difference between the excitement we might feel when we've decided to do something and the feelings that "speak peace to your soul" that Elder Rector describes. They are very different reactions. We should also be alert that both can occur. In fact, reactions of joy can follow the Spirit's confirmation as long as we identify which came first. Danger lurks when we feel our excitement *first* and then offer a quick prayer telling the Lord what we're going to do.

Protection against Less-than-Divine Answers

Finally, we can become anxious and worried trying to distinguish spiritual answers from our own desires, doctrines of devils, or even evil spirits. If we're not careful, we'll end up second guessing each internal sensation as we seek for truth. Thankfully, the Lord has provided a way to protect against these false witnesses.

Nephi describes the bravery of his father, Lehi, who stood among the wickedness of Jerusalem and declared the things he had seen. Jerusalem, at that point, was ripe for destruction, and the people were unwilling to be reminded of their sins. As Lehi preached repentance "they were angry with him" to the point that they "sought his life." However, out of this difficult situation, Lehi's family was spared and led to their promised land. In writing his account, Nephi is anxious to "show unto you that the tender mercies of the Lord are over all those he hath chosen." How powerful are the Lord's tender mercies? Nephi explains that, for the "chosen," those mercies will "make them mighty *even unto the power of deliverance*" (1 Nephi 1:20, emphasis added).

At the moment we plead with the Lord for answers, we desire, with all our hearts, deliverance. When we are bogged down in our own Winter Quarters, we grow anxious to break camp and find the promised blessings. We struggle, we plan, and we sort through the competing voices for the right path to follow. It is in those moments, as we prepare our hearts to receive direction, we can be "tenderized" by fully recognizing God's "tender mercies."

In other words, when we are in constant view of the Lord's tender mercies, we are less likely to be confused by phony imitations. They will sound shrill and self-serving in comparison. Our firm understanding of the Lord's daily interventions softens the heart and guards against deception.

Notes

1. Bruce R. McConkie, *Millennial Messiah: The Second Coming of the Son of Man* (Salt Lake City: Deseret Book, 1982), 44.
2. Joseph F. Smith, *Gospel Doctrine,* 5th ed. (Salt Lake City: Deseret Book, 1939), 373.
3. Dallin H. Oaks, "Alternate Voices," *Ensign*, May 1989, 27.
4. Milton V. Backman, *Joseph Smith's First Vision: Confirming Evidences and Contemporary Accounts* (Salt Lake City: Bookcraft, 1971), 164.
5. Hartman Rector Jr., "How to Know if Revelation Is from the Lord," *BYU Speeches*, Jan. 6, 1976, 1–7.

chapter ten

HELP FROM BEYOND THE VEIL

I WOULD NOT LIKE TO SAY ONE THING, NOR EXPRESS A THOUGHT, THAT WOULD GRIEVE THE HEART OF JOSEPH, OR OF BRIGHAM, OR OF JOHN, OR OF WILFORD, OR LORENZO, OR ANY OF THEIR FAITHFUL ASSOCIATES IN THE MINISTRY.

JOSEPH F. SMITH

*S*truggling once with a difficult problem, I prayed repeatedly but could not get an answer or direction as to what to do. In frustration, I determined to go to the temple, vowing to stay in the celestial room until I had my answer. In essence, I would stand on heaven's porch and keep ringing the doorbell until someone answered!

As I took my seat and waited for the session to begin, I slowly became conscious that the seat next to me, though empty, somehow felt occupied. I then had an immediate sense that someone unseen was sitting beside me. The feeling became so real that I hesitated to look. I had never before had such an experience and sat pondering what it meant. I understood a few moments later as I glanced at the slip of paper listing the name and information of the man I was doing the work for that night. I had a strong impression that the person sitting beside me was actually he. His work was being done that night, and he didn't want to miss it.

From that moment on, the session became a much different experience for me. It has been my sweet experience over the years to act as escort for a number of people going through the temple for the first

101

time. As I do so, I see the endowment session through new eyes, seeing and experiencing temple covenants as they might be seeing it. That night, I had a very similar experience. During the session, I attempted, in my head, to explain what was taking place. I paid closer attention to every commitment made and rejoiced with every promise given. It was a unique experience, one I do not expect to be repeated in my lifetime. The feeling lasted up to the moment I stepped into the celestial room, and then it was gone.

As I left the temple that night, I realized I hadn't dwelled on my problems at all. Nothing was yet resolved. I had missed my deadline. And yet I was as much at peace as if I had. My experience that night was not about me, nevertheless it blessed me tremendously. It reminded me again about the reality of the work going on in the Lord's house and the nearness of those whose work is being done.

As we appeal to the Spirit for answers, we awaken our deepest spiritual self. Surely, in the process of straining for gentle promptings, our spirit selves take note and are gratified with the additional fine-tuning we are going through. The gospel teaches us that the eternal part of us is far older than our mortal selves can comprehend in this life. For instance, while our natural man is concerned about worldly affairs, our premortal self cringes at the sheer shortsightedness of it all. Thus, the changing of our hearts is really a return to our most real self. It is a homecoming of the highest order.

Who among us does not thrill at the words of Eliza R. Snow:

> For a wise and glorious purpose
> Thou hast placed me here on earth
> And withheld the recollection
> Of my former friends and birth
> Yet ofttimes a secret something
> Whispered, "You're a stranger here,"
> And I felt that I had wandered
> From a more exalted sphere.[1]

Even investigators of the Church have an innate sense that they've truly wandered from a "more exalted sphere." This premortal imprint has led writers and philosophers, most of whom do so without revealed knowledge, to struggle to describe what they feel. In a sense, they have assurance without the knowledge. In ancient Greece, for instance, the idea of man's premortal life was commonly debated and widely believed.

Plato, as recorded in his famous dialogue *Phaedo,* answers a question of Socrates by saying,

"Your favorite doctrine, Socrates, that knowledge is simply recollection, if true, also necessarily implies a previous time in which we have learned that which we now recollect. But this would be impossible unless our soul had been in some place before existing in the form of man; here then is another proof of the soul's immortality."[2]

In fact, when Alex Haley was researching *Roots*, he traveled to a village where the concept of the spirit world was clearly understood. In *Roots*, Kunta Kinte is taught about those who live in each village:

"He [Kunta's father] said that three groups of people lived in every village, First were those you could see—walking around, eating, sleeping, and working. Second were the ancestors, who Grandma Yaisa had now joined. 'And the third people—who are they?' asked Kunta. 'The third people,' said Omoro, 'are those waiting to be born.' "[3]

This mortal earth, as it now exists, is not our home. We were nurtured elsewhere, taught and loved in the presence of heavenly parents. In the millennia before this life, we sought and received answers. We learned that "the glory of God is intelligence" (D&C 93:36) and that it would be our ultimate glory as well. To gain that intelligence, we came to earth.

A Glorious Venture

It is for this reason that our striving to better understand the promptings of the Spirit is actually part of a much deeper and far more glorious venture. At one level, we are simply trying to solve current problems. We seek help from Someone who knows our needs better than we do. When we connect with heaven, we reconnect with our eternal moorings. To call upon God and seek—again—His council is very familiar to our spirit selves. It is a process that will ultimately bring us back home.

As President Joseph F. Smith reminds us, "By the power of the Spirit, in the redemption of Christ, through obedience, *we often catch a spark from the awakened memories of the immortal soul, which lights up our whole being as with the glory of our former home.*[4]

The gospel has a familiar sound. The Spirit has a familiar feel. The answers we receive come from a familiar source. Humble seekers of truth have been hearing a familiar voice from the moment Joseph walked out of the woods following the First Vision. On the surface, the Restoration of the gospel, with angels, gold plates, and magic stones, has been laughed at by mainstream society from the beginning. Conversely, today's Church is filled with millions of people who have said, in effect, "I know these things. I recognize them; they are true! I don't know exactly *how* I know. I just do."

An old movie, *Random Hall*, features the following line, "The best of you, your capacity for loving, your joy in living are buried in a space of time you've forgotten."[5] And we know this is the case. We were spiritual beings before this life, and we seek to draw on that premortal propensity in our promptings, struggling to see in spite of the dark glass of mortality.

So, as we find our way in this life, we learn that we have a glorious past locked away within us. That wealth of warehoused spirituality can aid us as we bend our mortal will and soften our hearts in search of the Spirit. If our search for truth were aided only by our history, we would be eternally grateful to our Heavenly Father. But that is only half the story.

In addition to our premortal strengths, we are forever tied to the spirit world that lies in our future. It is filled with countless beings that love us and pray for our welfare. Mormon, looking toward our day, asks:

> Have angels ceased to appear unto the children of men? Or has he withheld the power of the Holy Ghost from them? Or will he, so long as time shall last, or the earth shall stand, or there shall be one man upon the face thereof to be saved?
>
> Behold I say unto you, Nay; for it is by faith that miracles are wrought; and it is by faith that angels appear and minister unto men. (Moroni 7:36–37)

The Ministering of Angels

In the Church, when we speak of the ministering of angels, we tend to think in terms of angelic visitations to prophets and Church leaders such as Joseph Smith. We also connect them to genealogical work, as any family history buff will quickly attest. However, far from prophets and temples, Aaronic priesthood advisors have young men turn to section 13 of the Doctrine and Covenants and read that they hold "the Priesthood of Aaron, which holds the keys of the ministering of angels" (D&C 13:1).

Some have asked why it is, given the prominent role that angels played in the restoration of the gospel, that the keys of the ministering of angels should be committed to the Aaronic priesthood, the preparatory priesthood. Shouldn't angelic ministering be a Melchizedek priesthood key?

Mormon himself clarifies the role and function of angels. He explains that he will "tell you the way whereby you may lay hold on every good thing" (Moroni 7:21). That way is explained below.

> For behold, God knowing all things, being from everlasting to everlasting, behold, *he sent angels to minister unto the children of men, to make manifest concerning the coming of Christ.* . . .
> "Wherefore, *by the ministering of angels,* and by every word which proceedeth forth out of the mouth of God, *men began to exercise faith in Christ*" (Moroni 7:22, 25, emphasis added).

In other words, throughout all ages, men and women have learned to develop faith through the teaching and ministering of heavenly messengers. As a result, they come into the kingdom through baptism.

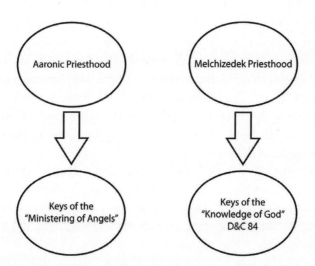

Nephi and Alma both understood angelic function. "Angels speak by the power of the Holy Ghost," Nephi says, "wherefore, they speak the words of Christ. Wherefore . . . feast upon the words of Christ; for behold, the words of Christ [often spoken by angels] will tell you all things what ye should do" (2 Nephi 32:3). Alma adds:

"And now, he imparteth his word by angels unto men, yea, not only men but women also. Now this is not all; little children do have words given unto them many times, which confound the wise and learned" (Alma 32:23).

When we are trying to understand what the Lord has in store for us, it should be comforting to receive knowledge and guidance that will "confound the wise and learned." In truth, the wise and learned—those who *think* they know what needs to happen—are often us!

Who Are These Angels?

Speaking at the funeral of James Adams, the Prophet Joseph Smith explained:

"The spirits of the just are exalted to a greater and more glorious work: hence they are blessed in their departure to the world of spirits. Enveloped in flaming fire, *they are not far from us,* and know and understand our thoughts, feelings, and emotions, and are often pained therewith."[6]

One of the misconceptions some members of the Church have concerning those in the spirit world is that those on the other side have little time or inclination toward those of us still in mortality. In actuality, the spirit world is very close by and its inhabitants clearly know our "thoughts, feelings, and emotions." They are so aware that they "are often pained" because of our actions. This suggests a much greater closeness between them and us than we might have considered.

And who are they? President Joseph F. Smith reminds us that "when messengers are sent to minister to the inhabitants of this earth, they are not strangers, *but from the ranks of our kindred, friends, and fellow-beings and fellow-servants.*"[7]

If we will allow it, this becomes one of the most comforting doctrines of the kingdom. When searching for answers, we can feel alone and forgotten. If we will, there can be great reassurance that there are those on the other side, those we loved in life, standing by to aid, to counsel, to guide.

One evening, while teaching a class on this topic, I noticed a young woman with tears in her eyes. Afterward I sat down and visited with her. Very emotionally, she revealed that her husband had died suddenly, six months earlier, leaving her with twin sons. The past few months, predictably, had been very difficult as she struggled to reconstruct her life.

In response, I felt impressed to tell her that she was not alone, that her husband was still very much concerned about their family. "In fact,"

I asked, "when was the last time you went somewhere with the boys?"

"Well, I took them to a play."

"Was your husband there?"

She looked closely at me and smiled. "He was," she replied softly. "I felt him next to me the whole time."

I then felt impressed to say, "He loves you and cares about you. He is still your priesthood leader and will help you along the way."

In retrospect I was amazed at what I told her. Certainly what I asked her was very personal and not something I would normally ask of a grieving widow. And yet, I felt impressed to share some things with her, which I hope blessed her with a measure of comfort.

Is this sister's experience unusual? In speaking on this topic to various groups of Latter-day Saints, I have been touched and enriched by those who have come forward afterward to share very similar stories about love and support coming from those on the other side of the veil. From these experiences I've come to believe strongly that one day we will be pleasantly surprised to learn just how often we were aided from the spirit world.

If this is the case, we can also assume they know when we are in search of an answer to prayer. Elder John A. Widtsoe made this additional reassuring statement in that regard: "Those who give themselves with all their might and main to this work receive help from the other side, and not merely in gathering genealogies. *Whoever seeks to help those on the other side receives help in return in all the affairs of life.*"[8]

The most comprehensive statement on this topic came from President Joseph F. Smith. In his later years, President Smith was weighed down with illness and with the deaths of several members of his family. In addition, his sensitive spirit mourned the senseless slaughter of "The Great War" taking place in Europe as well as the great flu epidemic that killed many thousands. It seemed he was surrounded by pain and death on all sides.

President Smith spent the last two years of his life in almost complete seclusion and, by his own admission, close to the veil much of the time. In fact, the wondrous revelation on the spirit world, received a month before his death, is now recorded as section 138 of the Doctrine and Covenants. It was delivered by his son at the October Conference in 1918, given, ironically, to a half-filled tabernacle due to the flu epidemic. That revelation gave us an increased appreciation for and knowledge about the workings and activities occurring in the world of spirits, especially concerning the visit of the Savior following His death and resurrection.

Perhaps less well known, though, is his masterful and emotional address delivered eighteen months earlier at April Conference, 1916. That talk, which he aptly named "In the Presence of the Divine," gave an intimate and telling look at those beyond the veil and their "solicitude" for those still toiling in mortality.

In it, President Smith explains:

> [Those in the spirit world] see the dangers that beset us; *they can comprehend, better than ever before, the weaknesses that are liable to mislead us* into dark and forbidden paths.
>
> They see the temptations and the evils that beset us in life and the proneness of mortal beings to yield to temptation and to wrong doing; *hence their solicitude for us*, and their love for us, and their desire for our well being, *must be greater than that which we feel for ourselves.*[9]

Can we picture, for a moment, those we have loved who have passed from this life? Imagine their love for us increasing as their eternal understanding grows. At critical moments in our life, could they be standing close by while we search for answers? Can you also sense how their veiled encouragement might feel as we develop the courage to follow our promptings? And while we may try to guess what is going on just beyond the veil during our struggles, we should not have to wonder *if* something is happening. Grasping the power of President Smith's statement, we can take great comfort in the idea that we are never alone in our trials and struggles.

They are aware of us and are "solicitous" for our welfare. We may not know in this life exactly what form that support will take. But, in a Church restored literally by heavenly hands, we shouldn't limit their help in any way!

Finally, our connection with heaven reconnects us with two powerful sources of spiritual power. On one side, we brush up against familiar guidance that filled us in our heavenly home. The Holy Ghost unlocks dormant knowledge learned eons ago. In this life, while it often feels as though we're learning gospel truths for the first time, in reality, we are most likely recovering knowledge we first gained as premortal spirits. That unlocking process will flood us with former knowledge and help us understand our promptings.

We are also aided by the wealth of love and support that exists for us on the other side of the veil. In many ways they understand us better than we understand ourselves. Certainly, their love for us is greater than the love we have for ourselves. What form their support takes we may never understand in this life. But our thoughts and prayers and gratitude should be directed to those who have preceded us. The spirit of Elijah will turn the hearts of the children toward their fathers so that both will be blessed.

Years ago, a good friend of ours was visited by two older Maori women from New Zealand. They had flown to Utah to spend some time at the Church's genealogy facilities. To make room for them, our friend moved her two boys into another room and put these two humble sisters up in the boys' bunk beds.

One night, after a long day searching family histories, these two sisters were sound asleep. Suddenly, the sister on the bottom bunk awoke with a start to find a man dressed in brilliant white standing beside the bed. She looked closely at him. Then, filled with simple Maori faith and understanding, this sister pounded on the bed above her. "Hey," she called out, "your father is here to see you." She then rolled over and went back to sleep. The appearance of her friend's father was a common enough experience that she was not surprised when it happened.

Said another woman who had recently moved to Utah from a very small branch in a developing country: "You know, there are people here who have never seen an angel! Isn't that amazing?"

As our spiritual knowledge grows and our faith increases, we strive more diligently to trust more in heavenly knowledge than in our own. We then develop our willingness to follow that inspired counsel. Those on the other side may, at times, be involved in bringing us the answer we seek. Their increased love and caring should be, for us, a source of warmth and strength as we strive to obey that counsel.

Notes

1. "O My Father," *Hymns*, no. 292.
2. *Dialogues of Plato*, trans. Benjamin Jowett (Chicago: Encyclopedia Brittanica, 1952), 228, quoted in Edwin Brown Firmage, "Recovering and Discovering Truth" *Ensign*, Apr. 1981, 38.
3. Alex Haley, *Roots* (New York: Doubleday, 1976), 18, as quoted in Brent L. Top, *Life Before* (Salt Lake City: Deseret Book, 1988), 1.

4. Joseph F. Smith, *Gospel Doctrine*, 5th ed. (Salt Lake City: Deseret Book, 1939), 15–16.

5. As quoted in Truman G. Madsen, *The Highest in Us* (Salt Lake City: Bookcraft, 1978), 16.

6. *History of the Church*, 6:52.

7. Joseph F. Smith, *Gospel Doctrine*, 5th ed. (Salt Lake City: Deseret Book, 1939), 435.

8. "Genealogical Activities in Europe," *Utah Genealogical and Historical Magazine* 22 (July 1931): 104. As quoted in Boyd K. Packer, *The Holy Temple* (Salt Lake City: Deseret Book, 1980), 252, emphasis added.

9. Joseph F. Smith, "In the Presence of the Divine," Conference Report, April 1916, 2–3.

chapter eleven

LOFT MOMENTS

PERSONALLY, I AM ALWAYS READY TO LEARN—
ALTHOUGH, I DO NOT ALWAYS LIKE BEING TAUGHT.
SIR WINSTON CHURCHILL

*L*earning to recognize the workings of the Spirit means also committing to follow its dictates. As part of our growth on this earth we are tried and tested—even while doing what we've been asked to do. Father Abraham stands out as the great example in this regard. From Egypt to Issac, his life was filled with blessing and sacrifice—the one dependent on the other. And before we get too comfortable viewing Abraham's challenges across the safe span of millennia, we should pay close attention. As tests go, his trials may be familiar.

"You have all kinds of trials to pass through," warned the Prophet Joseph Smith, "and it is quite as necessary for you to be tried even as Abraham, and other men of God. God will feel after you, he will take hold of you and wrench your very heartstrings, and if you cannot stand it you will not be fit for an inheritance in the Kingdom of God."[1]

That should be a sobering statement. The Lord has indicated that where much is given, much is expected.[2] Greater light brings greater accountability. "I will give you answers," says the Father, "but I expect you to do what you have been prompted to do. And because you have received the answer—and you know you did—you are left without excuse. To move forward will bring you happiness and joy. To draw back will leave you comfortless. Now, here is what I had in mind . . ."

Someone once remarked that each person in the Book of Mormon stands as an example or a warning. The same is generally true of the other standard works as well. One example I place on par with the Abrahamic sacrifice is the story of Elijah and the widow in Zaraphath. We do not know her name, but we revere her example.

Due to the wickedness of the people, Elijah had sealed up the heavens. Rain did not fall for three years. For a while he was fed by ravens until even the brook he lived by dried up. The Lord then told him to go into the city, where a woman had been commanded to take care of him. We do not know the nature of the Lord's command to her, nor do we know if Elijah would understand her situation. We only know he met her in the city.

> And when he came to the gate of the city, behold, the widow woman was there gathering of sticks; and he called to her, and said, Fetch me, I pray thee, a little water in a vessel, that I may drink.
>
> And as she was going to fetch it, he called to her, and said, Bring me, I pray thee, a morsel of bread in thine hand.
>
> *And she said, As the Lord thy God liveth, I have not a cake, but a handful of meal in a barrel, and a little oil in a cruse; and, behold, I am gathering two sticks, that I may go in and dress it for me and my son, that we may eat it, and die.* (1 Kings 17:10–12, emphasis added)

In my mind, I have tried, in a small way, to picture the full measure of her situation prior to meeting Elijah. According to the law of Moses, as a widow, she should have been taken care of by her husband's family. This does not appear to be the case here, because, instead, she is left alone, trying to provide for her son. In addition, whatever has been the source of her provisions is no longer available. She stands at the very end of her options, with no other resources left. As she goes to bed the night before, she has resigned herself to this one last, small meal. She will give this one last cake to her son and then prepare for their deaths.

Elijah's initial request would seem, on the surface, to be a pretty selfish act. That she "make [him] thereof a little cake first" might have caused most of us to question his motives. However, since the Lord had "commanded" her, she may have been blessed with some level of spiritual insight. Had she been told he was coming? Did she somehow see a prophet in spite of his rough appearance and have the Spirit whisper that somehow she would be blessed? In any case, her decision to first give Elijah their last meal is an astounding act of courage and faith by any measure.

Then, just when it appears that the miracle of the oil and meal would be the end of the lesson, the Lord presents both the widow and Elijah with one more challenge. Within days, this courageous woman finds that her son, who she thought was going to starve to death and then was preserved, has now died. This sudden tragedy, coming right after the miracle, appears to catch both the widow and Elijah by surprise.

> And [Elijah] said unto her, Give me thy son. And he took him out of her bosom, and carried him up into a loft, where he abode, and laid him upon his own bed.
>
> And he cried unto the Lord, and said, O Lord my God, hast thou also brought evil upon the widow with whom I sojourn, by slaying her son? (1 Kings 17:19–20)

For Elijah, this "loft moment" is the test that comes after a miracle has been received. The lives of this widow and her son had been preserved. She had risked everything to take care of a prophet only to be rewarded with her son's death. "Why this?" Elijah asked. "Why now?"

In response to his faith and pleadings, Elijah's prayers were answered and "the soul of the child came into him again, and he revived."

Each of us have our own "loft moments," those times when we retreat to our own loft and question why the Lord appears to hand out curses in the midst of blessings—to bless us and then take those blessings back. Like Elijah, we then have to reach down deep into our faith and draw on a measure of strength in order to gain answers from heaven.

If we are not careful, we can find ourselves looking for the "fairness doctrine" in life, that part of us that demands that everything should be "fair." One night, my then thirteen-year-old daughter proceeded to detail all the ways in which kids around her had nicer clothes, more freedom, less responsibility, and so forth. She concluded the familiar teenager rant with "It's just not fair!"

"Whew," I exclaimed, "I was getting worried. If your mom and I were being fair, we might be doing the wrong things. Thank you. I feel much better!" *She* didn't, of course. At that age, it's a difficult concept to grasp. Even adults are not immune to "fair-itis." *Keeping the commandments should prevent me from having loft moments, shouldn't it? I'm trying to do everything right. And I see members of the ward who just seem to sail right through. It's not fair!*

True, it is not fair. For the widow standing before Elijah, for Abraham as he binds Isaac at the altar, and for the exhausted handcart Saints who were rescued *and then* had to climb Rocky Ridge, obedience generally doesn't exempt us from trial. If we are not prepared, however, we may find ourselves stunned, recovering in our personal loft moments, and tearfully pleading with the Lord to find out what happened.

A mother speaks in Church and says: "I'm grateful for my husband's job and the success my kids are having in school. We have been so blessed!" I'm still waiting for the testimony that begins with: "Well this month, Lucy was diagnosed with cancer, and I lost my job just after the car broke down. We've been so blessed!" We still have a tendency to paint those moments when things are going well as blessings and trials as something else.

Arza E. Hinckley was nineteen when he left Nauvoo, driving a Church team across the frozen Mississippi to Mt. Pisgah. When the call came to form the Mormon Battalion, he agreed to go and have his military pay given to the Church. During the long walk toward San Diego, he became ill, refusing the Missouri doctor's poisonous treatments. Finally, halfway across New Mexico, he was unable to proceed farther. He was then assigned to a "sick detachment" heading back to Sante Fe. The sick detachment was denied permission to winter at Sante Fe and so they were forced to hike over the mountain and into Pueblo on frozen feet and swollen joints. As soon as the snow melted, they made their way into the Salt Lake Valley, arriving just four days after Brigham Young.

Arza had been in the valley for only a few weeks when he joined Brigham Young's party returning back to Winter Quarters. President Young was anxious to reunite all the apostles so the First Presidency could be reorganized, and Arza was anxious to rejoin his younger brother (President Hinckley's grandfather), who was somewhere on the trail. On the return trip, for the first time in a thousand miles, Arza was finally able to ride a horse and was no longer walking. His swollen joints, still aching from malnourishment, disease, and the brutal journey, were finally getting a well-deserved rest.

It is easy to understand Arza's anger and frustration when, a few days into the journey, his horse was stolen by Indians somewhere across Wyoming. His anger was compounded when a group of Indians rode into camp a few days later, one of them riding Arza's horse. Spotting his horse tied up and in camp, Arza quickly found his army rifle and started off to get his horse back. One of the brethren, watching all this unfold, alerted Brigham Young.

"Young man, what are you doing?" Brigham called out.

"I'm going to get my horse," Arza replied.

"Son, let it go," Brigham directed.

After a moment of reflection, and fully cognizant of the long journey still ahead, Arza shrugged and replied, "You're the boss!" and put his rifle away. In later life, he would claim that Brigham's command had stopped him from starting a Mormon/Indian war. He shuddered when he thought about it. The reality, though, was that he was forced to walk the rest of the way back to Winter Quarters. In his writings, there was never another word about losing the horse, just gratitude for being stopped in his attempt to get it back.[3] His unwavering obedience to the Lord's prophet remains part of our family heritage today.

Arza's obedience in following a prophet's voice did not result in immediate comfort or relief from his trials—in fact, it brought about just the opposite. It would be easy to say that some of his difficulties were not fair. But he obeyed and passed along a legacy of faithfulness that is cherished generations later.

For us, obeying a prompting may have a similar effect. Moroni, worried that his lack of writing skill would cause future readers to condemn his words, received specific guidance from the Lord regarding his concerns. "If men come unto me," the Lord explains, "I will show unto men their weakness." (Ether 12:27)

Weakness, in this case, carries a double meaning: 1) humanness, fallen natural man, and 2) our own individual flaws and challenges. Either way, the Lord assures us through Moroni that as we draw closer to the Lord and stand more within His light and knowledge, we will be shown, much more clearly, the full extent of our shortcomings. This could be one of the reasons many investigate the Church and then run! Few things are more painful than being given a clearer understanding of our flaws. They are the last thing we'd really like to see more clearly. Like my teenage daughter would say, "That's not fair!"

And yet the Lord's plan of happiness does not call for us to run from our weaknesses. In fact, the Lord reminds us that "my grace is sufficient" (Ether 12:27). It is this grace and His eternal promises that bring comfort to our loft moments. Life is not fair, trials can seem unbearable—but the Lord's grace and Atonement will ultimately right every wrong and bless us far beyond what we deserve. To us He whispers:

> Fear not, I am with thee; Oh, be not dismayed,
> For I am thy God and will still give thee aid
> *I'll strengthen thee, help thee, and cause thee to stand,*
> Upheld by my righteous, omnipotent hand
> The soul that on Jesus hath leaned for repose
> I will not, I cannot, desert to his foes;
> That soul, though all hell should endeavor to shake
> I'll never, no never, no never forsake.[4]

Certainly Elijah, as he understood the desperate circumstance of the widow, could have excused himself and her for demanding so much from someone in such desolate circumstances. Perhaps he could have used the sealing powers he possessed to fill the barrel and cruse of oil *before* she baked the last cake. In other words, there were a number of ways to make her decision less painful—but then she would have missed the experience of the empowering the Lord intended for her.

Skeptics of the Church use the phony argument of "Well, if you'll show me the gold plates or an angel, then I'll believe." It is the same logic used by those who chafe against "Church rules" by complaining, "The Church is too hard! Make it easier!" Not wanting to sacrifice, they look for the easy way out. But, as one writer suggested, that would require the Lord to love them less.

One evening, while working with a group of clients out on a ropes course, I placed a contentious couple up on two thirty-foot perches in separate trees. They were each attached to a belay line to keep them safe. High up in the trees, they were forced to confront the constant name-calling and bickering that had plagued their marriage for years. Ironically, with their emotions elevated by the height and by fear, they argued even more.

Finally I had heard enough arguing. I securely tied off their safety lines and informed them we were leaving. They both looked down at me in shock. I then took the rest of the group off to do another activity.

A few minutes later, I quietly crept back, hiding behind a tree where

I could listen. Thinking they were completely alone, they continued to blame one another. Then, seeing their plight, the tone changed. I finally heard the wife say softly, "we're not going to get down from here until we figure something out . . ." Her husband agreed. Slowly they began to talk more honestly.

After they had talked for a while, I then stepped out from behind the tree and complimented them on their insights. I helped them apologize and make some heartfelt commitments to one other and their marriage. Later, the wife confessed just how much the experience had helped change their marriage and that it wouldn't have happened had I not left. It was only as she saw the two of them physically separated and stuck high in the trees that she could finally see the real state of her marriage.

A life lived heroically, in spite of difficulty, will affect generations. That we lived is a given. How we live is watched closely by those after us. *An empowered life becomes a consecrated life.* It can be used by the Lord to further His purposes and bless the lives of others.

This type of celestial "tough love" was clearly understood by C. S. Lewis.

> We want, in fact, not so much a Father in Heaven as a grandfather—a senile benevolence who, as they say, "liked to see young people enjoying themselves," and whose plan for the universe was simply that it might be truly said at the end of each day, "a good time was had by all."
>
> God has paid us the intolerable compliment of loving us in the deepest, most tragic . . . sense. We are . . . in very truth a Divine work of art, something that God is making, and therefore something with which He will not be satisfied until it has a certain character. Thus it is perfectly natural for us to wish that God had designed for us a less glorious and less arduous destiny; *but then we are wishing not for more love but for less.*[5]

At the end of the day, our promptings, the answers to our prayers, will send us on journeys the Lord has in mind and help us fulfill our goal to become more like Him. We cannot begin to know where that path will lead, but we are comforted by the knowledge that we will be filled with the power to accomplish it. When we ask for answers, we covenant to follow them. In return, we are filled with power to aid us on our way.

Notes

1. Joseph Smith, as quoted in Harold B. Lee, Conference Report, April 1963, 88.
2. See Luke 12:48 and D&C 82:1–4.
3. Journal of Arza Erastus Hinckley, BYU Special Collections.
4. "How Firm a Foundation," *Hymns*, no. 85.
5. C. S. Lewis, *The Problem of Pain* (New York: Touchstone, 1996), 35–36.

chapter twelve

THE PEACEABLE WALK WITH THE CHILDREN OF MEN

YOU CANNOT SIN SO CHEAP NO MORE.

HEBER C. KIMBALL

hile teaching an institute class called "The Gospel and the Productive Life," I looked hard for a quote the class could memorize and repeat at the beginning of each class. I wanted the quote to be a reminder, in a nutshell, of the importance of incorporating the gospel of Jesus Christ in everyday actions. The one I finally chose comes from a talk by President Spencer W. Kimball in 1977. Said he: "If we live in such a way that the considerations of eternity press upon us, we will make better decisions."[1] His thought encapsulated our need to make daily decisions with a more eternal perspective. At the end of the semester, it was gratifying to hear one of my students recite this quote in his sacrament meeting talk prior to leaving on his mission. He had made a better decision.

I have come to know that this entire process—loving the Lord, having our hearts changed, seeking divine answers, recognizing quiet promptings, and moving ahead with courage—is the essence of God's great "plan of happiness" (Alma 42:8). It is the path that will ultimately bring us to celestial glory.

In President Kimball's talk quoted above, he also quotes Brigham Young, who once was asked if there was one thing he would wish for the Saints, what would it be? President Young thought for a moment and then replied that he would give them "eyes with which to see things as they are."[2] Seeing ourselves and the Lord as we really are helps us to make those critical daily decisions that determine our eternal destiny.

These daily decisions highlight the sacred responsibility of those entrusted with heavenly guidance. President McKay summed up the gospel this way: "The purpose of the gospel is . . . to make bad men good and good men better, and to change human nature."[3] Gaining revelation, through prayer, is essential to that journey from bad or fallen man to good or redeemed man. It enables us to make the final step from redeemed man to empowered man. The final phrase in President McKay's statement suggests that there is yet one more aspect in this journey: "to change human behavior." That is no small task!

At Christmas, I've always enjoyed the classic *A Christmas Carol* by Charles Dickens. In it, we watch Ebenezer Scrooge's nighttime of transformation as directed by his former business associate Jacob Marley. He is first visited by the Spirit of Christmas Past, reminding him of his childhood struggles and joy. The Spirit of Christmas Present brings him a sense of regret as he sees Christmas through those closest to him. Finally the Spirit of Christmas Future fills him with dread as he sees what will happen if he continues on with his same behavior. In the end, a transformed Scrooge is led to plead, "I'm not the man I was!"[4]

It has been said the purpose of prayer is not to change God. It is to change us. If we pray with the humility and trust that invite real answers, a transformation occurs in us. We simply will not be the men and women we once were. By opening ourselves to His solutions, we set ourselves on a different path, one of heaven's choosing. That inspired path prepares us to become the people He intended all along. And with it, we are then prepared to serve.

The idea of changing human behavior also begs a question: whose nature is changed—ours or that of others we meet? If our goal is to work toward a pure-hearted Zion, the answer is clear: Yes! In such a setting, both are changed. Even more, the act of lifting another ennobles us at the same time.

When Hurricane Katrina battered and then flooded the city of New Orleans, we watched with a sense of detached horror. The magnitude of the disaster was unbelievable. Then, just as the waters were receding, the call came for our stake in Dallas to mobilize and send a large amount of men down to the general area for cleanup. Several days before, we sat waiting at the stake center as the stake president received our exact assignment during a phone call. Afterward, he walked to the podium, sighed, and said softly, "we're going to New Orleans."

Two days later we drove down into New Orleans, pitching tents in the vast tent city in front of the stake center there. While driving through a particularly hard-hit area, a man asked if we could help his mother clear out her house. Following him, we drove over to a nice home that had been mostly under water for two weeks. For hours, as his mother watched, we rolled her entire household down her front steps and out to the curb. This included her grand piano (she taught piano lessons), her gilded gold mirror, as well as her treasured china. Even her most prized possessions were tossed out onto the street as trash.

At one point, I tearfully turned to her to express my condolences. This elderly lady just smiled at me and responded, "Son, it's okay. It's just stuff. We'll be all right." Only later did her son reveal that he had sought us out because, years ago, they had fed the "Mormon Elders" dinner on a regular basis. How grateful I was that we could, in a small way, repay them for their kindness at the same time I had a son serving a mission.

President Kimball understood the "double blessing" involved in the Lord's work:

> I have learned that . . . when we are engaged in the service of our fellowmen, not only do our deeds assist them, but we put our own problems in a fresher perspective. . . . In the midst of the miracle of serving, there is the promise of Jesus, that by losing ourselves we find ourselves.
>
> Not only do we "find" ourselves in terms of acknowledging guidance in our lives, but the more we serve our fellowmen in appropriate ways, the more substance there is to our souls. . . . Indeed, it is easier to "find" ourselves because there is so much more of us to find.[5]

The scriptures are full of reminders that our mortal existence was never intended to be a game of solitaire. A small list includes:

"Forgive us our debts as we forgive our debtors" (Matthew 6:12).

"It is not good that the man should be alone" (Genesis 2:18).

"We without them cannot be made perfect" (D&C 128:18).

"The hearts of the children shall turn to their fathers" (D&C 2:2).

King Benjamin wanted his newly converted people to understand that their *personal* testimony and their *personal* righteousness were only the beginning and would not save them. In order to maintain those mighty changes, much more was expected.

"And now . . . for the sake of retaining a remission of your sins from day to day, that ye might walk guiltless before God—I would that ye should impart of your substance to the poor, every man according to that which he hath . . . administering to their relief, both spiritually and temporally, according to their wants" (Mosiah 4:26).

Gaining answers to prayers is intended to help us serve. If we are to walk the "peaceable walk with the children of men" (Moroni 7:4), we cannot camp out at home, basking in the glow of our righteousness. As we cast off the natural man and experience the fundamental change of heart, we are drawn to assist others as they have their natures changed too. Such a transformation in our nature is a call to serve. Conversely, failure to serve can be an outward sign that we are still resisting those critical changes.

In 1903, President Joseph F. Smith was called to testify before the US Senate during the Smoot hearings. The purpose of the hearings was to determine if the senate should seat its first Mormon senator, Reed Smoot. In reality, the hearings were a skeptical referendum about the Church and its former position on plural marriage. For this reason President Smith was called to Washington to testify before the senate committee.

Despite his humble and honest responses, President Smith was widely ridiculed in US and European newspapers for years after his testimony. Newspapers ran outlandish political cartoons using him to caricature life in Utah. Despite this avalanche of mean-spirited abuse, President Smith calmly pressed forward, without guile or offense, in helping the Saints focus on the right priorities of this life. He wanted them "fixed in their minds, with a determined resolution" (Alma 47:6) to live a Latter-day Saint life, which he described in this way:

> But the men and women who are honest before God, who humbly plod along, doing their duty, paying their tithing, and exercising that pure religion and undefiled before God and the Father, which is to visit the fatherless and the widows in their afflictions and to keep oneself unspotted from the world, and who help after the poor; and who honor the holy Priesthood, who do not run into

excesses, who are prayerful in their families, and who acknowledge the Lord in their hearts, they will build up a foundation that the gates of hell cannot prevail against; and if the floods come and the storms beat upon their house, it shall not fail, for it will be built upon the rock of eternal truth.[6]

Senator Smoot, who was also serving as an apostle, followed President Smith's example. After he was finally seated in the US Senate, he reacted to the rancorous opposition with humility and meekness. He reached out to others in kindness and friendship. His example helped offset much of the misunderstandings and ignorance so prevalent during his confirmation, and he went on to become a leader in the Senate.

The call to serve is rarely a call to ease. It is rarely a call inside our comfort zone or field of expertise. Shortly after my call as bishop, I sought out a new Relief Society president. After prayerful consideration, I called her and her husband in. She looked expectantly at her husband, waiting to see what he was being called to. She was startled when I explained that the Lord had a calling for her. She was even more shocked when I extended the calling to be Relief Society president. In response, she stammered and stuttered. What I could gather was that she didn't feel qualified and that she felt most of the women in the ward were more qualified than she was. After listening, I responded with, "Sister, all I know is that the Lord first called me as bishop, and now he wants you!"

After she took a few days to think about it, this good sister came back, accepted the call, and went on to be a great Relief Society president. Because of her humility and lack of ego, she won over several sisters who wouldn't have responded any other way.

In addition, we should also have confidence that our call to serve will constitute a personalized challenge, one designed just for us. For instance, our lay ministry in the kingdom will require us to work with people we never would have known otherwise. True, we will often serve with fellow Saints that bless our lives and become our closest and dearest friends. Along the way, we will also serve with those who are difficult to serve, those who reject our service, or those whose need is so great as to draw the spiritual wind completely out of our sails.

Others, heeding their own call, will receive us as part of their stewardship. Our job, our sacred responsibility, is also to be willing to be served. We will be blessed by inspired teachers; we will be blessed by unprepared teachers; we will be blessed by terrified teachers—each one with something to teach us. Certainly, the receiving end of some service can be among the most difficult things we are called to do in the Church. "Some leaders are sent to lead us," J. Golden Kimball is supposed to have said, "and some are sent to try us."

It is easy to be a Saint when we are not faced by adversity or trial. The measure of who we've become is the grace with which we handle those who wrong us. How we treat others, regardless of how they treat us, defines if we are truly walking the peaceable walk. The promptings of the Spirit will lead us to treat people with the love and concern demonstrated by the Savior in every aspect of His mortal ministry.

The story of the gospel is the story of service and sacrifice. There are many additional examples that could be cited that cause us to evaluate our own level of commitment to those around us. I would like to finish with two moving examples that demonstrate a complete understanding of the Christlike love we all should be seeking.

Example 1

In 1984, a film crew followed Hugh Nibley to Egypt to film him as he explored ancient Egyptian sites. Late one afternoon, near the end of the shoot, they rested in the shade of some trees. As Brother Nibley looked out at the heat of the afternoon sun, he began openly reflecting on the life of Abraham. He described one experience, according to the ancient Midrash:

> It was a hot day. It says it was a day like the breath of *Gahinum*, like the breath of hell. So Abraham sent his servant Eliazer out to search the surrounding area, but Eliazer found no one. Still worried that someone might perish in the burning heat, Abraham finally went out to search himself. By the end of the blistering day, he still had found no one. When he finally returned to his tent, there were three people waiting for him. It was the Lord and the two with him. . . . It is then that the Lord promises him Issac, as a reward for what he had done, you see. The supreme offer. He'd gone out to look for his fellow man in that dusty hell, all alone. Eliazer couldn't find anyone, and he said 'I think I can find somebody.' Well, he found something. He found the answer to the thing he'd prayed for all his life: his son Issac. . . . It's a very moving story.[7]

Example 2

When my daughter was a junior in high school, we felt prompted to accept a job offer from a good friend in Utah. The day we started the long drive from Texas to Utah was a particularly tearful one for her. We were concerned about the effect of such a move on all our kids but were especially prayerful for her, given that she was on the high school tennis team and firmly part of a group of friends. The day I dropped her off at her new high school, she was apprehensive and quiet. Again I prayed the same prayer every parent prays at such a moment: that good friends would find her and that she wouldn't be alone.

Then a miracle happened. An inspired group of seminary council kids spied the nervous girl from Texas and immediately welcomed her with open arms. They loved her, accepted her, and took her everywhere with them. Tears about the move were quickly forgotten, and lifetime friendships were forged. Their incredible warmth and selflessness filled us with endless gratitude and awe.

In the end, striving, searching, and pleading for God's loving guidance calls on our most inner self. It awakens and stirs that ancient part of our soul still wistfully standing near the veil, yearning to return. There are moments we "see through the glass darkly" (1 Corinthians 13:12) and then turn back to the harsh realities of daily life. Deep down, we are all more homesick than we know.

When we learn to love, really learn to love, we seek the Spirit as we seek the sun.[8] It guides us in our service; it answers our prayers. It becomes a lifeline of inspiration even as the wickedness of the world crowds around us. When that inspiration comes, it then parts the curtain of darkness and illuminates us with the glory of our former home. It is, as the beautiful words of *Redeemer of Israel* remind us:

> As children of Zion, good tidings for us.
> The tokens already appear
> Fear not, and be just, for the kingdom is ours
> The hour of redemption is near
> Restore, my dear Savior, the light of thy face
> Thy soul-cheering comfort impart;
> And let the sweet longing for thy holy place
> Bring hope to my desolate heart.[9]

Notes

1. Edward L. Kimball, ed., *The Teachings of Spencer W. Kimball* (Salt Lake City: Bookcraft, 1989), 25.

2. *Journal of Discourses*, 3:221.

3. From the film *Every Member a Missionary*, as acknowledged by Franklin D. Richards in Conference Report, October 1965, 136–37.

4. Charles Dickens, *A Christmas Carol*, Stave 4.

5. Spencer W. Kimball, "Small Acts of Service," *Ensign*, December 1974, 2.

6. Joseph F. Smith, *Gospel Doctrine*, 5th ed. (Salt Lake City: Deseret Book, 1939), 7–8.

7. Text from the film documentary *Faith of an Observer*, 1984. Also quoted in Boyd J. Petersen, *Hugh Nibley: A Consecrated Life* (Draper, Utah: Greg Kofford Books, 2002), 332.

8. Truman Madsen, "Hugh B. Brown—Youthful Veteran," *New Era*, April 1976, 17.

9. "Redeemer of Israel," *Hymns*, no. 6.

in conclusion

*P*rayer is something we share with every other individual on the planet who looks heavenward for help. It is a universal principle shared by most cultures and religions. At the same time, the sacred communication between man and God is also intensely personal. The counsel we receive is privately and lovingly tailored to match our knowledge, maturity, and needs. This uniquely divine dance yields up critical counsel, individualized and meant to be understood only by us.

For this reason, the principles we've discussed constitute general guidelines, culled from the combined wisdom of inspired prophets and leaders who learned and grew from their own strivings in the Spirit. Their knowledge gives us a blueprint that helps us as we strive to better communicate with heaven.

At the same time, we cannot be so completely bound by lists and rules—trying to get our answers "the best way"—that we end up relying on a "cookie cutter" approach. As we discussed earlier, our unique set of spiritual gifts and personalities helps us shape how we respond to things of spiritual import. Just because someone we admire receives personal revelations a certain way, we would be shortsighted to assume their way is the "preferred" way or the best way. Equally damaging is the idea that any other way would be "second rate" or less inspired. We can never lose sight of the idea that revelation from God is just one aspect of an overall relationship with Him.

Second, in the years I've taught this topic, in many different settings,

I've been struck by a clear insight of my own in relation to those I've met: Latter-day Saints, by and large, do not know how good-hearted and well-intentioned they are. By our nature, we tend to focus on areas we need to change. We fuss, we fume, we adjust, we repent, we change, we slide back, and we try again. But always we keep moving forward, trying our best to do the right things for all the right reasons. This is a process we will carry into the spirit world, for weaknesses not corrected in this life become part of the polishing in the next. Certainly we are an eternal work in progress.

Thus, in the midst of this trying to improve, we might lose sight of how unique this process makes us, given the world in which we live. The profane and the wicked seem to dominate the headlines and the evening news. They are the loudest voices seeking attention and air time. At the same time, the good-hearted of the earth wake up each day, simply trying to live better lives than they did the week before and do so without fanfare or news coverage. Because there is no story there, there are no headlines in the epic personal struggles to do the right things for the right reasons.

It is no surprise, then, that you who are the good-hearted—and imperfect—of the earth desire to counsel with the God you love. You yearn for closeness and reassurance and help in difficult circumstances. You kneel and pray precisely because you believe He loves you and will answer you when you ask. And when you are unsure, as you struggle to discern between promptings and personal thoughts, you demonstrate a desire not just for answers but also for the living waters that flow from the true source. At those moments, you know that water from your own backyard well will not do!

It is for all these reasons I believe, with all my heart, that we receive far more answers to our heavenly petitions than we realize. Our lives and our ongoing desires combine to bring forth Heavenly Father's love and therefore His answers to us. Nothing brings Him greater joy than pouring out blessings upon our heads as we seek them. Unfortunately, if we are not careful, many of those answers are left unheard because we expected something other than what we received.

It is also for this reason that we should not make prayer so difficult an exercise that we spend needless time and energy worrying about the mechanics of this most natural and loving relationship. As we talked about in chapter one, there are certain elements we know instinctively.

We know He loves us, that He is anxious to answer us. We also know that when He speaks to us, it comes through the still, small voice, leaving a feeling of love and peace afterward. The more we follow that voice, the more we learn to trust it and the greater happiness we find. And we know the alternative—that doing life on our own terms brings only chaos and regret.

In addition, ongoing and heartfelt gratitude for our blessings allows us to look more closely at the multitude of tender mercies that grace our lives continually. I know that when I stop and truly look, I am always in awe of the things He has done for me. It is always overwhelming. During these examinations, I am more able to see the Lord's divine handprint in the midst of seemingly random acts, guiding and directing the events around me. I've found that the final result of His interventions does not guarantee life without pain; on the contrary, it often seems to increase it. But I've come to know that His way does assure my growth and development, leading me ever more surely toward my potential.

One other aspect that is sure to call forth my gratitude is that crystal clear understanding that when I look forward to a "judgment day," I have earned exactly nothing. My behavior and obedience, if fairly judged, would yield an eternity outside His presence. But, astonishingly, I will not—nor will you—receive that judgment. Many of us will stand, at a future day, clothed with glory and eternal lives, bathed in celestial glory. It is what God intended for us all along. And that future is possible for us because of love and mercy and an unfathomable sacrifice.

If we catch the smallest sense of the depth of that mercy, if our hearts begin to fill with those swelling feelings of love, I believe we pray differently. We feel our souls reaching out to Him, seeking to know what it is He wants for us. We then covenant to do what He wants us to do. In return, we receive what we need, now and in the eternities. And as we understand and are filled with gratitude, how can we do otherwise?

about the author

Kevin Hinckley is a psychotherapist and life skills coach. He is a facilitator with the LDS Addiction Recovery Program and sits on the board of directors for ANTHEM and Strong Families Dallas, a non-profit organization and advocate of marriage and families in North Texas. He is a frequent speaker with Church and youth groups as well as at Campus Education Week at BYU and BYU–Idaho.

Kevin is the author of two previous books, *Parenting the Strong-Willed Child* and *Burying Our Swords*.

Kevin graduated from Brigham Young University in 1985 with a master's degree in counseling and an emphasis in organizational behavior. He also did doctoral work in counseling psychology.

He and his family live near Dallas, Texas.